Katie,

You've come a long way - I'm honored to be a guide in your journey. Keep unleashing that Majikal Power within! ♡

Nicole Majik

the BEAD SMITH® mini macramé board

designed by Anne Dilker

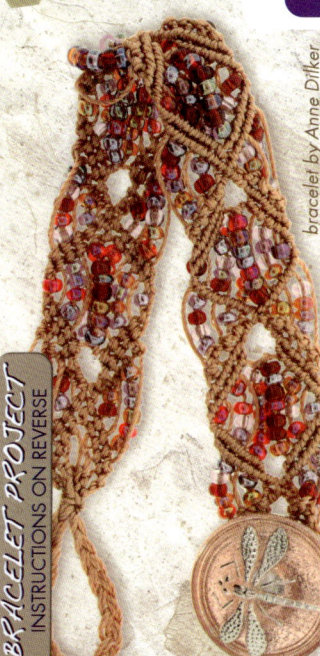

A new twist on an old classic!

- Cord management made easy... Specially designed notches on all sides hold cords securely in place!
- Ideal for multiple cord projects, including macramé, Shamballa bracelets, decorative knotting & more
- Smooth surface won't snag cords
- Lightweight & small – excellent for travel
- 6" x 9" grid for easy measuring
- Self-healing – use with pins without damaging the surface

BRACELET PROJECT INSTRUCTIONS ON REVERSE

bracelet by Anne Dilker

PATENT PENDING

Item Number: MWB10

For how-to instructions and project ideas, scan QR code or visit: www.beadsmith.com/macrame

www.beadsmith.com • Carteret, NJ • Made in China. Not a toy. Not intended for use by children under 15 years.

There are literally hundreds of jewelry patterns you can make using just 4 or 5 very basic knots and any smooth surface coating will yield a lovely bracelet or necklace. As any seasoned knotter will tell you, cord management is always an issue with macramé. This board is specifically designed to help you corral the cords. It's okay to use pins if you'd like, you'll find that this board will hold your pins more tightly than the old style boards.

Beaded Macramé Bracelet

Materials list:
- Tex 210 S-Lon (sample made with Copper)
- Size 8/0 seed beads (I used BeadSmith Vineyard mix)
- 20mm button (sample used Czech glass)
- Clear drying super glue
- Sharp scissors
- Straight pins (optional)

Step 1: Pull six 72" lengths of S-Lon. Find center and back off about 1". Make braid (or sinnet) to form loop. I made a simple 3 warp braid using 2 strands of cord for each warp.

Step 2: Finish the loop by wrapping one piece of cord around all and tie with a half hitch. Repeat the wrap and half hitch a second time.

Step 3: A) Put the loop in one of the notches at the top of the board. Place all 12 ends in the bottom notches. B) Since this project is worked in two halves (the left side and then the right side) I tend to divide the placement into two groups of 6 with an empty notch or two in between the groups. Not necessary, but it can be helpful.

Step 4: Begin by making a series of square knots. Starting with the 2 outside cords on the left side, tie a square knot. Then using the center two cords on the left side, tie a square knot. Lastly, using the inner most two cords on the left side, tie a square knot (for a total of three knots). Repeat on the right hand side.

Step 5: Using the innermost cord from each group (the two center cords) tie a square knot and then another square knot.

Step 6: A) Using the outermost left cord as the core, tie a row of diagonal half hitches over the remaining five left hand cords. Place the core cord on the inside of the left hand group. B) Repeat on the right side.

Step 7: Repeat Step 6.

Begin the Pattern...
Step 8: Using the second most inner cord tie two half hitches around the first left hand cord. For the veteran knotter, these are known as vertical half stitches.

Step 9: Slide two seed beads onto the third cord in the left hand group and tie two half hitches around the second cord in the group.

Step 10: Use the 4th cord to tie 2 half hitches around the 3rd cord.

Step 11: Slide six beads onto the fifth cord and use it to tie two half hitches around the fourth cord.

Step 12: Use the sixth cord to tie two half hitches around the fifth cord.

Step 13: Repeat Steps 9-12 on the right hand side.

Step 14: Using the innermost left hand cord as the core cord, tie a row of diagonal half hitches. Return core cord to the outside of the left hand group. Repeat on the right hand side.

Step 15: Repeat Step 14.

Step 16: Tie a square knot using the two center cords. These are the innermost cords; one from the left & one from the right.

Step 17: A) Use the outermost left cord as the core cord for a row of diagonal half hitches, then slide one bead onto the second most outer cord and tie two half hitches over the core cord. Use this cord to tie 2 half hitches over the core. Slide 4 beads onto the 4th cord and tie 2 half hitches. Tie 2 half hitches with the fifth cord. Slide 7 beads onto the sixth cord and tie 2 half hitches. B) Repeat on the right hand side.

Step 18: Tie a square knot with the center two cords (one from each group).

Step 19: Repeat Steps 17 and 18.

Step 20: Repeat from Begin the Pattern (Step 8).

Step 21: Once the desired length has been made, finish by tying a square knot using the inner two cords on each side (use four cords to tie the square). Slide the button onto a group of six cords, then use all twelve cords to tie a square knot. Glue the knot; let dry; then trim the ends.

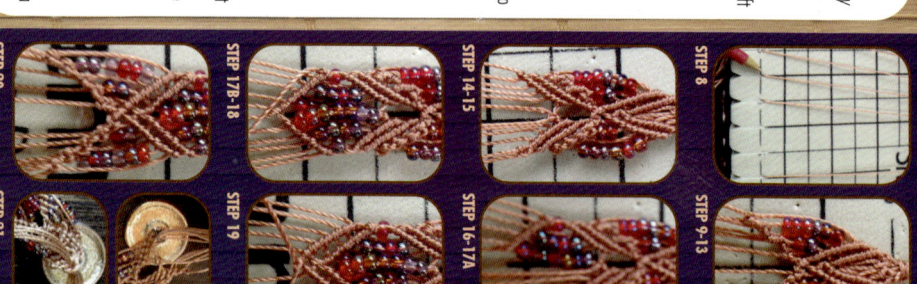

Don't Be Invisible Be Fabulous
Volume 6

A Mile In Her Shoes

Compiled by

Dorris Burch

FAB FACTOR
Publishing

Don't Be Invisible Be Fabulous, Volume 6:
A Mile In Her Shoes

Copyright © 2021 Dorris Burch

All rights reserved. No part of this book may be reproduced or transmitted in any form or by any means, electronic or mechanical, including photography, recording or any information storage and retrieval system without written permission from the authors and publisher.

Each author in this book retains the copyright and therefore all rights and subrights to her individual chapter, used herein with her permission. Each author is responsible for the individual opinions expressed and statements made.

Published by Fab Factor Publishing
Tinley Park, IL
www.thefabfactor.com

ISBN: 978-0-578-93461-7

Cover design, layout, and typesetting:
Fab Factor Publishing

Cover photo: Charles Taitt

This book is for every woman who has had a vision that others might not understand. It's for every woman who is sick and tired of playing by the rules. It's for every woman who has known she was meant for more and has waited far too long for someone to give her the permission she thought she needed.

CONTENTS

INTRODUCTION xi

I'M READY TO OWN MY SPACE
Kelly Fox 17

HOW I BECAME A WELLBEING WARRIOR
Connie Warden 41

BECOMING EPIC
Angela Witczak 55

A LIFE PERCEIVED IS A LIFE RECEIVED – EMBRACE YOUR BECOMING
Nicole Majik 77

FEAR
Amber Trail 113

SILVER LINING LEGACY
Tia Bottum 129

I CAN SEE CLEARLY...NOW
Kaylee McDonald, ND 147

HONOR - HOPE – HAPPINESS
Susan Lataille 161

ACKNOWLEDGMENTS 192

MEET THE FABULOUS DORRIS BURCH 193

The fabulous Dorris Burch

INTRODUCTION

Sometimes I still doubt my own power, not sure why but it happens. Then something wakes me back up! I have had several moments like that for me putting this book together. And just like any other obstacle in life, I can decide to CHOOSE and CREATE joy because happiness begins within you, not outside. But first I have to ask myself. "How did this even happen, and why did I CHOOSE it, why in fact was I not allowing for anything other than this?"

If you're not asking these sorts of questions, and INSISTING upon a clear and immediate answer from higher self, soul, God, all of the above, then guess what? YOU are gonna get to keep experiencing the same lesson over and over again until you get it. And all of the trying in the world can't stop that, because hey – the thing of not getting what we want only happens when there's still something we need to know or understand.

I had to remind myself, as I want to remind you, it takes time to heal emotional wounds fully and completely.

However, as EmpressPreneurs, we have the power to choose and create joy. YOU are your greatest source of happiness. Joy comes in the way you show up for yourself, pivot, and reevaluate. By turning to outlets like journaling and meditation to just observe your feelings (without judgment), you can better manage your emotions and use them to channel your deepest desires.

When I ask the Divine what the theme title for this book was going to be… my soul heard "A Mile In Her Shoes" … how fabulous as I think so many women look at other women and make assumptions about who they think she is and what she's doing without knowing the path she is walking in life.

What I realized was God knew this message needed to be amplified during such a time as this. That amidst this global pause we're coming out of in many ways, many women are taking a moment to dive deeper into finding their soul purpose. Wondering how they could make an even BIGGER contribution to the world.

God is constantly supporting us in ways that aren't always obvious, we just need to trust in His divine timing. Remember, faith is the evidence of things not yet seen!

If we've seen anything during such a time as this, it's the desperate NEED for feminine leadership. We need more women stepping up and FABULOUSLY LIVING from a place of authenticity, passion, and femininity. Your energy, my energy, the power of the collective energy can transform the entire global vibration from fear, lack, and uncertainty to love, joy, and abundance.

Take a moment to just… BREATHE. Center yourself and remember: everything is happening for you, not to you.

I wanted to remind you what an important time this is for you to… RISE UP.

Yes there can be fear and uncertainty…. AND yet there is also opportunity, servitude, and people out there that are looking up to YOU for guidance and comfort.

You have a role to play and a mission to fulfill. You are being called to own your lane of feminine leadership like never before!

But either way,

regardless of what's going on,

coming at you,

thrown your way,

by life

by business

by a pandemic

the economy

or love

or you!

You ALWAYS still have the power of choice to choose.

I will say this to you… Don't doubt your power - I won't doubt my power either 😀

Remember –

Don't Be Invisible. Be Fabulous!

The Fabulous Dorris Burch

Kelly Fox

I'M READY TO OWN MY SPACE

My first memories are when I was 3 years old. This was the first time I felt "less than" or invisible. My mom was pregnant and I could no longer fit on her lap. I loved sitting on her lap and getting to be closer to her. She was everything to me. My caregiver, yes, she is my mom, but she's also the one who saw me, held me, and comforted me. I barely remember this time of my life, but I definitely remember how I felt after my brother was born. I lost some of that feeling of being special to her. Like I was less seen, less important. I know now as an adult and with having six kids myself that this is not so, but then it felt very true.

When my brother was born (the first boy after a long line of 8 girls) he temporarily paralyzed my mom. He came home two weeks before she did, and when she did come home, she came home in a wheelchair. I was mad at him. This little baby not only took away my mom, but he hurt her too. I felt powerless to change the situation I now found myself in. To make matters worse, because Kent was the first boy, he got all new stuff. We were in the newspaper with the heading of "When eight is not enough". My great grandfather who lived with us, and who had always treated me special even over my sisters, was now doting over him. The man who once saved a place for me beside him, who saw me and cherished me, now was preoccupied with someone else. I felt pretty invisible, to say the least, by almost everyone. But, being seen by my mom was always a desire that I worked for from that time on.

At first, I didn't care if she saw me positively or negatively. I would throw fits and hide from her and test her to have her prove that she did see me. That didn't work in my favor. She forgot me everywhere. There was even a commonly known joke at our community theater of, "Terry, you forgot Kelly again". She would take me to school shopping and look for things for my sisters instead of for me. She went back to work when I was 4 or 5, so I had a babysitter. From the time I was five on, she was a working mother. I know that is not a bad thing; I am grateful for her desire to work and her ability to do so. It's just that she was a work-a-holic. As an amazing kindergarten teacher, she gave her all to her kids at school. Though by the time she got home, she was wiped out, out of energy, and therefore out of patience. As a kid craving attention, this was a bad combination.

The one place my mom and I connected was on the stage. We both loved to do plays at our local community theater. I did every summer show, and during the school year, I was in a pre-show youth group that she co-directed. The theater was not only a place my mom saw me but also a place where others saw me too. I loved the stage. My theater family was where I felt like I belonged, more than my own family. I loved being there. My first play was "Carousel" when I was four years old. I never had a big part, yet I was always seen for my attitude on stage and for my smile. I was often told I stole the show.

As I got older, I became more self-conscious. I was a chubby kid, and I knew it by comments and efforts by my mom to help me lose weight. I remember weighing myself at my grandmother's one weekend I was staying over there, which I did often, and just begging the scale to not go over one hundred pounds. When it did, I thought, "Okay, now it's all downhill from here. This is my life. I'm the fat kid." I was in 6th grade. I started to not want to be seen. I tried to blend in and not be anyone special. I was good with being last chair saxophone in the band in junior high and high school. I went for leads in plays halfheartedly. I wanted so badly to fit in and be normal. That wasn't going to be my story, not anymore.

This is when my depression really started to kick in. I had horrible self-talk, beating myself up relentlessly. I felt worthless and therefore, anyone could treat me however they wanted to. In eighth grade, I went around a whole day at school saying that when I got home, I was going to kill myself. One friend took me seriously. She brought me home with her and made me talk to her. I really didn't have a reason to justify my dramatic claims so I said that I liked a boy that didn't like me. Really, I was just miserable, no reason, it was just how I was. This was my normal. She made me call the boy. I was so embarrassed that I started to put a long knife down my throat. I really don't know what I was thinking. I did wish the boy liked me. We were good friends and I wanted to be wanted by him, or by anyone really. He was special to me. But to kill myself over him not liking me? I don't think so. But now he thought that, and I couldn't imagine going back to school the next day. So, I grabbed the closest thing. I didn't even think about what could have happened. I guess 12-year-olds don't really think about those things. Luckily, she stopped me, that would have been a horrible way to go.

I'm not trying to say that I had this awful life, because I didn't. I had a loving theater community, great friends, and my family really did love me, even if I couldn't always feel it or see it. That was a filter that I had created as a young girl, and it took years to let go of it. I grew up with amazing sisters that I looked up to and saw as super talented, smart, and easily liked by others. I didn't feel like that myself at all. I felt ugly, stupid, and hard to love. I later would call these my "complexes". Yet now I know they were heavily ingrained lies of fear. They kept me from loving myself, and by so doing, not feeling anyone else's love.

I DIDN'T VALUE MYSELF

The summer before my freshman year, I had my first serious relationship and could finally say I had a real boyfriend. It was exciting and scary, and I couldn't believe he liked me. This was the start of a long practice of trying to please a man, caring about his needs far beyond my own. I had thoughts like, is he satisfied? is he happy? I still have this challenge now to a certain degree.

I remember shortly after we started "dating", my dad drove him home and I walked him to the door. He leaned forward for a kiss. I thought it would be a simple peck, but what he did was a full-on French kiss! I was caught by surprise. We hadn't kissed that way before, and my dad was there in plain sight of us. I kissed him back so I didn't leave him feeling any kind of discomfort or rejection. But as I turned to walk back to my car and my dad, I was super uncomfortable and scared about what my dad would say. He looked at me, as I avoided his eyes, and said, "Kelly I don't think you are ready to be doing those kinds of kisses." I quickly responded with, "I know dad, I'll talk to him about it." And fortunately, he left it at that. He was a pretty amazing dad.

My father was the one person who always saw me. He was the kind of person who took the time with people, truly cared for people, and always wanted to please you. He would carry us to bed at night if we fell asleep on the couch. He would take me to school in the morning once I started high school, with my sisters. He had eight daughters and we all felt special to him. We all had individual relationships with him. We all felt equally loved by him. Thinking back on that now as a parent myself seems like an impossible task. The one he didn't love was himself. Shortly before he died, we did a family night and he gave us all a self-esteem test to take. He got the lowest score out of all of us. I was the second-lowest, which surprised him. In this, my father and I were quite the same.

My freshman year went by quickly. I was in the band, I played the saxophone, and I hung out with my friends. I didn't get great grades, basically a C student. With ADHD and a general challenge with school, that was not an esteem booster. This continued into high school and my early 20's. I didn't value myself so no one else did either. I had one or two really good friends, that I really showed everything to. They knew my ups and down to a point. No one could see all the darkness or I would scare them and make myself even less desirable. I hid that part of me from everyone. I didn't have anyone that I could trust enough with that. My sister who was the closest in age to me was one who got the brunt of my insecurities. I would constantly tell her that she loved others more than she loved me. I tested her as well, for her to prove or at least say that she loved and valued me more than anyone else. I think this was very exhausting for her. She would get easily annoyed by me and my constant need for reassurance. One time I was insisting to go with her and her friend somewhere and we were going on her bike. I was sitting on her handlebars, and she pushed me off. I don't think she was trying to hurt me; she just really didn't want me to go. I fell in the street and scratched up my knees pretty bad. She took me into the bathroom to clean up the dirt and blood. She told me she was going to get something to help me and left the room. She didn't come back. She went off with her friend. Leaving me there bleeding and in pain. This is something I still bring up from time to time today, in a joking manner. I was devastated though at the time. It was not my sister's responsibility to address my inner feelings of unworthiness, nor anyone else's. Though I felt like it was, and I blamed her and other members of my family for it.

My dad though, I held as my rock. He always saw me, even though he had 9 children. He made me feel loved and seen and not broken in any way. When I wanted to be seen, it was usually by him. In high school, I ditched quite a bit, and before my best friend got a car, we ditched on foot. I lived about 9 or so blocks from school, and we would dodge the "ditcher car" all the way to my house. I don't know if there was really someone out there driving around looking for kids who were attempting to leave school, but that was what I was led to believe, and we definitely tried to avoid it. Once, we were almost to my house, about 2 houses away, when we discovered that my dad was home. He caught us. We tried to hide, yet he had already seen us. Instead of taking us right home, he understood my situation of not wanting to go to class because of a missing assignment, and he devised a plan. My friend and I took turns alternated working on my homework with riding our exercise bike. It sounds so funny now, and we still joke about it from time to time, yet at the time we complied. After lunchtime, he took us back to school, and my work was done. He was like that: slow to anger, and out of the box with his way of addressing situations. Not a black and white thinker. He was strong and loving and just about perfect to me.

That is why what he did on December 18th, was so surprising and devastating. He had told us about a week or so before this that he had done something stupid and there would possibly be consequences. I thought maybe he and my mom would split up. I for sure wanted to go with him if it came to that. But, on the night of our church Christmas party, Heather, my older sister of three and a half years, came to ask us to come outside, because my mom had something she wanted to tell us. I had the most awful feeling during the walk to the parking lot. On the way, Heather asked the bishop to join us, and I knew this was not an announcement of a surprise trip to Disneyland. When we got to the car, Heather turned around and said, "Dad shot himself, and he's dead." My whole world shattered. I remember almost fainting into my bishop's arms. I don't remember much after that for about 30 minutes. I remember saying over and over again, "Not my daddy, I need my daddy" until my mom told me to shut up, we all needed him, not just me. I just wanted to die too.

The next year or so was a blur. I seriously don't remember much of it. I guess I went along pretty dazed and oblivious to the life around me. I remember about a year and a half later asking my mom if this meant my dad was going to hell. She explained to me that all the good my dad had done before this one mistake would not be for nothing, and that he was not going to be judged for one act above all the others. This brought me some comfort, and I felt a sense of relief, that not all was lost. I would have dreams about him coming to me and reassuring me of his love and that "the guy upstairs was helping him to feel better". This was encouraging too. This whole experience left me though with a sense of unworthiness and abandonment issues. That I wasn't good enough for him to stay around and that he would leave me to the disapproval and dislike of my mother. She didn't see me and she wasn't proud of me and she seemed to see me as a nuisance, as I thought, whether it was true or not. I felt like I would never be loved like he loved me again. I would never be looked at and valued like he did again. I kind of floated through life at this point. I would go from not caring about things to then wanting to make him proud of my actions. I fluctuated between emotions of anger, shame and disbelief.

    My first year in college my sister and I were walking to our next class and we saw a depression screening. We thought, why not, let us go see how messed up were we. I took the assessment, and it came out that I was severely depressed. The lady giving the test was surprised that I could get myself out of bed every day. I was astonished by the results. I didn't think I was that bad. I had good days, and didn't everyone feel sad or bad about themselves? I guess that wasn't the case. Not everyone went around waiting fondly for the day their life would end because that would mean a break from their existence and the exhausting life it was. I eventually went to see a doctor and started on a medication; it stabilized my mood for a while. I had a tendency to go off-and-on my medication. This was a pattern for the next 20 or so years (until I was diagnosed with bipolar 2). I hadn't really been committed to taking it consistently forever. I use to hate the idea of always needing something to be "normal". I struggled through my life, trying to explain my depression, and then trying to hide it. I was very talented at faking it. I even got dubbed "Bubbles" at church camp. When I was named, I thought, "Wow, they really don't know me". I could make you laugh and distract you from the rest, and it worked with most people.

I CAME BACK A DIFFERENT WOMAN

When I was 21, I went on a mission for the Lord with my church. I knew God loved me and that the Savior sacrificed for me his life, yet I didn't feel worthy of it. I wanted to repay them with the giving of 18 months of service. I was scared to leave my family for that long with no contact other than letters and two calls a year. I didn't think I was able to be that disconnected from my only support system. I made it through with the daily letters from my mom and the occasional letter from family and friends and the power of prayer. I had an amazing time, and I learned a lot of lessons, from those I taught the gospel, from my companions, and from my mission leaders. I came back a different woman. I knew of my resilience and my love for the gospel of Jesus Christ. I also knew that I was capable of more than I had previously given myself credit for.

A few months after arriving home, I met my future husband. Jay and I had a short relationship before we got married, about 7 months to the wedding. I felt like I knew him very well and that he knew me. I told him about my depression and all my baggage. I didn't want there to be something he didn't know and then for him to change his mind. Later I found out that he was not as forthcoming. We had a rough beginning. I had a lot of expectations, and so did he. I was disappointed quite a bit; married life was not what I had pictured. Also, I had never been so responsible for expenses and adult-type stuff, nor he. We struggled to find our place, and we were always chasing that perfect place and situation for us to be able to have this so-called perfect situation. We moved around a lot—we'd spend 4 months here and 6 months there. We kept looking for a place we could afford that wasn't so far from his work and that felt like home. About 7 months into our marriage, I got pregnant with our first child. Jay felt the need to settle down and get a house. We picked my hometown because there I would have the most support with our coming child. This meant though that I would only basically see him on the weekend. Though I had my best friend and my family to keep me company. Before this, we were living about 3 hours away and I was driving almost every weekend to them. This way I would be with them more and he would drive home every weekend. It was a strain on our marriage, yet I had the support with a new baby.

We only had the house for about a year until we felt like it was time for something new. We were back at the short-term chase of the perfect place. This led us to Jay quitting his job and looking for something in my hometown for him to do. Being a computer programmer didn't give him many choices in a rural country town. He struggled to find a job, and nothing paid what he was previously was making in San Jose. I ended up taking two jobs—one at a woman's gym part-time and the other at a sunglass store in the mall—to help with bills. I also got pregnant with our second child. He eventually got a job delivering newspapers, which he started at 2 a.m. I could see this weighing on him and destroying his self-confidence.

He kept looking for a job and unbeknownst to me, he started looking anywhere for work. He was given a position in Atlanta, Georgia. This seemed so far away and unknown. I couldn't imagine going this far away from everyone I knew and my entire support system. He was determined to go. He told me, "I'm going with or without you." Being 5 months pregnant with our second child, I didn't see how I really had a choice. He went before us and started his job while I continued to work and raise money for our move. It was hard to be away from him and working while I had an 18-month-old. My best friend helped out with babysitting, which was a great blessing. Though, with Jay away, I felt like I had lost that source of love he provided to me.

During this time, Jay's father died suddenly from a heart attack, and he completely withdrew. I didn't know what to do. I knew how it felt to all of a sudden lose your father, yet he responded in a different way than I did. I discovered quickly that everyone deals with grief differently. After the move it didn't improve; things actually got worse. I was now a mother of two little ones, and he was mentally and emotionally distant. He was faking it through and I could tell. I played that game well. He was secretive and withdrawn and started acting out of character. I was lost as to what to do. I constantly brought it up and shared my concerns and my desire for him to come back and be engaged. I don't think this supported him or the situation. Eventually, about 4 years into our marriage and after about half a year in Georgia, he told me over the phone one day that he no longer loved me.

I was blown away and slammed by the reality of my worst nightmare. I bought plane tickets for the kids and me that day, and we were gone by that night. I was in shock and thought the only way to survive was to go home. When he came home from work to take us to the airport, he was quiet. There was no begging me to stay or discussion on how this was going to work or what was going to happen. He just let me leave. On the plane, when my son realized that his dad would not be joining us, he started to cry, and I almost lost it right there on the plane. I was barely keeping it together as it was. I was going on complete adrenaline. It was a horrible flight. We had to do a layover in Phoenix and we almost missed our next flight. I was starting to see how life would be with no one to help out.

My sister and her husband picked us up from LAX around 1 or so in the morning. We were exhausted, to say the least, yet I could not sleep. The restlessness and questions were swirling in my head. I couldn't believe I was in this situation. Never did I think we wouldn't be together forever. I figured we would just always work things out, no matter what. That wasn't the case for him, and from that time on it wasn't the case for me either. I called him around 4 or 5 o'clock in the morning that same day because I hadn't slept yet. It wasn't so early for him; he was on eastern time. I cried and questioned and begged for him to take it all back, for him to say he really did love me. He didn't.

The next few weeks I walked on eggshells. I didn't want to call him too much or keep him on the phone too long. I would bring up my pain or when we might get back together. I never gave up hope though. I was just waiting for him to realize that he did love me and want our family together. It was the 4th of July, about 3 weeks since I had flown away from him, that I had… had enough. I let him have it. He was missing his daughter's first 4th of July, and it was almost our wedding anniversary. I couldn't keep in my anger and disappointment anymore. I told him that he was lying to himself and making up all these excuses to justify his choices and that he was going to lose the best thing that would ever happen to him. And thankfully he woke up and agreed. We went back to Georgia a week later. I decided if we were going to work, that I couldn't throw this in his face or use it to manipulate him. It would come up from time to time because I wasn't pretending that it didn't happen, yet I wouldn't use it as a weapon. I'm not going to tell you that our marriage was better after that. We continued to struggle this way for another few years. And even today, the thought of walking away from it all still comes to my mind from time to time. Though for the most part, we are happy, and we now have 6 kids, and we are going on 20 years of marriage.

TRUSTING MYSELF

The biggest thing that happened in Georgia, since we only ended up living there for 18 months before we moved back to California and my hometown, was that I found Fearless Living and Rhonda Britten. This was the beginning of my discovery to myself. It has been a long process, and I am and will be on it until I'm gone from this world. My journey has been so far one of miracles. It started with a morning reality show called Starting Over. If you are not familiar with it, the show was about 6 ladies living in one house and working with two life coaches and one psychiatrist, and they worked out their issues right there on the screen. I thought they were brave and courageous and amazing women. I thought that there was no way I could do what they were doing. There was no way I could go on TV and tell the world about all my issues. For one, it was too exposing and embarrassing, and second, I could never out my mom like that. At this time, I was still blaming her for most of my issues (Sorry mom). I watched every morning as they did an exercise to work through their stuff and find answers to their problems. I was inspired. And, then my luck changed, and the coaches and doctor went on a mall tour. I was determined to be there. There I felt drawn to one of the coaches, Rhonda Britten. I stood in line for her signature, and I took a big risk and signed up for a book group of her book Fearless Living, with women I didn't know at all. This was so scary; it was a "Die" in Fearless Living terms. I had never stepped so far out of my comfort zone. Almost every class at first, I didn't want to go. And then I began to change. My thoughts started to change, and I started to see some of the lies I had been living by.

    I started to see the small box I had put myself in. I started to see all the limitations that I had put on myself, and I started to see more clearly who I was and how capable I really was. I began thinking, if this could help me this much, then what could it do for others that I could share it with. I had been a psych major before I was pregnant and left school, and it had been my wish to do something in that field, and maybe here was my chance to support others that struggled like me. I started looking into what it would take to be a life coach too. One of the pre-requisites was to work with a pre-approved coach from the community of Fearless Living coaches. I hired Bindu Wiles. She was amazing for me. She held me accountable in love and asked me the hard questions. She put me on my journey of setting boundaries and seeing what I wanted and also what I was expecting from myself and others. We discovered some of the stories I was telling myself, and she made it easier to see when others were acting out of fear as well. This was very helpful for the times when Jay and I separated. I attribute Fearless Living with keeping my marriage together, even now. For instance, when I let Jay have it on that 4th of July, a lot of what I said was the language I had learned from working with my coach. I challenged all the stories he was telling himself and that he was trying to convince me were true. Yet they weren't true; actually, almost the opposite was true. And it started to show me what could happen when you use the tools I was learning and start to make changes.

Over the last almost 16 years at this point, I have changed a lot. Just ask Jay and my mom. I see my beauty, my strength, my capability, my intelligence, my resilience, my greatness. I can now own my Rock Star status. Was it easy? Heck no! I did it one day at a time, and I wasn't consistent either. Really, if I can do this, anyone can. I know people say that all the time, yet it really is true here. I did become a life coach, and I do support people to love themselves more, to see their worth, and to own their power to create the life they want to be living. I do that by doing the things daily that I ask them to do. I write 5 acknowledgments and 5 gratitude's a day. I have an intention for my life, which is, "Today I am willing to practice trusting myself more". Trusting myself is the key for me to step out of fear and into taking risks, growing, and having the life I want. It may be something different for your life; compassion, courage, or authenticity to name a few. Acknowledgments and Gratitudes—or as I call them, A&Gs—have given me more confidence in my life, have built up a stronger belief in myself, and have shown me how capable I am at making anything happen.

As I challenge myself every day to write down 5 things I did the day before, it makes me show or prove to myself that I did think of myself, I did take risks, I did keep my commitments to myself and others, I did what I said I would. As I do this every day, or more often than not, I engrain into my head that "I can". I prove fear a liar every day! And on the days that I doubt that I can look back on all the acknowledgments, I have written before and remind myself of all I have done and how far I have come. I have gone from wanting to hide to shining my light. Not only am I writing my story here, I am also a podcast host, I give live and virtual workshops, and I have a group coaching program. I even do one-on-one coaching too, from time to time. I really love the group environment. I am visible, and I challenge myself to be more and more visible. I can still fake it from time to time, I still am bipolar, yet I show my real self to a lot more people, and I am honest and up-front about my mental illness. I don't shy away from talking about suicide. In fact, I actually hold a fundraiser for our local efforts of suicide prevention every year in honor of my dad. I am an open book in most cases.

This came by doing the daily actions and being willing to say yes! Saying yes to myself, to my desires, and to taking risk after risk. My comfort zone is pretty big now in areas where it used to be very small. I used to not believe in myself very much or think that there was anything needed from me being here. I have spoken of that a little already. I didn't think I was capable of anything. One of the Fearless Living tools that I used at the beginning and still do is asking myself, "Am I making it up, or is it true?" This tool gave me permission to change my mind or write a new story. I used to think that I could never do things on my own, that I always needed someone else's help. I challenged that belief several times before I started to overcome it. During 2020 I have challenged it again and again. My spirits have gone through a rollercoaster during this time. Yours may have too. When I came upon anything, I would ask myself this question. "Am I making it up, or is it true?"

"I can't see anyone." I can Zoom.

"I can't do workshops if we can't be in the same room." I can do them virtually.

"I'm stuck at home with all 8 of us with nothing to do." We have created new routines for our family that include a family-involved meal schedule, a family game night weekly, family spiritual time once a week, and scripture reading time as often as we can fit it in, aiming for daily, and we do church services with each other on Sundays. This has helped me and my family to grow individually and together.

Use this question and see what it will do for you. I remember the first time I was able to look in the mirror and tell myself that I am beautiful. It felt so awkward and vain. Now I can say it out loud and to others, and it only feels weird a little bit. I am continually getting better at loving myself, trusting myself, and acting on what I want to make happen for myself, my family, and my business. These are things I never dreamed of happening. Like changing my mindset, believing in my capability, and seeing my own beauty; none of these things felt possible to me. I have now created workshops and facilitated them. I have created a 12-month coaching program, which involves 2 workbooks, 2 PowerPoints, 2 classes a month. We are now in our 7th season of our podcast, Fearless Generations 12 Steps to Freedom. I have 6 amazing kids that are amazing human beings, and I am for the most part happy. That really is something I thought I would never have. Because I do the little things each day, a great life has emerged. I'm not saying I don't have bad days or that my fear doesn't win from time to time. We, including me, will be on this journey for our whole lives. Yet, I get better at it one day at a time, one step at a time, and one risk at a time. If you are reading this, then I know that you are on a journey as well. You may be where I am or somewhere different. Wherever you are is where you are meant to be, and I am honored if my story has supported you in any way.

The End

ACKNOWLEDGMENTS

I would like to thank my family, my husband Jay, and my kids Daniel, Irisa, Lily, Hazel, Liam, and Griffyn. I'd also like to thank my mom Terry Sayre and the creator of Fearless Living Rhonda Britten.

ABOUT AUTHOR

Kelly Fox is a mother of 6 and has been a Fearless Living coach since 2008. In her process of learning how to own her space, she learned how to help others own theirs. She is a speaker, workshop and group coaching facilitator, podcaster, and managing contributor in the On Purpose With Purpose community.

ABOUT MY BUSINESS

When working with me, you will give yourself permission to be you, step fearlessly into the spotlight, and attract the recognition you want! I will support you with seeing clearly your purpose and together we will design your path to freedom.

Website
www.KellyLynneCoaching.com

Facebook Personal Page
www.facebook.com/kellysayrefox

Twitter
www.twitter.com/kellyfox

Instagram
Kelly Lynne Coaching

THANK YOU OFFER

I'd love to meet you and see if I can support you with your journey.
Contact me here:
https://app.acuityscheduling.com/schedule.php?owner=17713059&appointmentType=15323946

Connie Warden

HOW I BECAME A WELLBEING WARRIOR

"While growing up we fatten our personalities and starve our essence" - Unknown

This essay is part of my story, of how I went from being a ninja (camouflage expert) to loving my being-ness, enough to allow myself to be seen in the world and to become a Well-Being Warrior.

I connected with Dorris Burch, the author of this book, right from the beginning. I resonated with her brand of "Don't Be Invisible, Be Fabulous".

For the first part of my life I was doing just that; being invisible. I am glad to say this is not true anymore.

The part of my personality that I fattened the most, was to learn how to stay hidden.

Fattening the qualities of not trusting me or the world and not feeling I had a sense of value (low self-esteem).

The essential qualities I starved were confidence, trust, and self-love.

There was one essential quality that I did not starve. This one quality has, and is, helping me feed my essence more and more each day.

That essential, innate quality is curiosity.

I believe we all have essential or innate qualities of the soul. Love, joy, intelligence, confidence, gratitude, compassion, etc. Curiosity is also an essential quality. I know, I have 2 granddaughters and I clearly see their innate curiosity!

I am always filled with a deep sense of awe every time I play with them, reminding me how much joy and love I felt when raising my own son and daughter. As I look back over my life, I realize children have always been an integral part of my world.

I was the third sibling out of eight. Really, until I was 12 years old, my mom was always pregnant. I loved helping her take care of the smaller children, showing them new things, making them laugh and smile, and changing their cloth diapers (ok, I did not love that so much).

My father was a sign of the times. To him, discipline was best taught through physical consequences and being hit for infractions, both large and small, was commonplace in our home.

I recently realized that as a young child, it was this aggression that set me on my path of trying not to be seen and to undervalue my spirit.

I was a small kiddo and could fit in tight places where no one would think to look for a child. I would often seek out these spaces in search of something that is so rare in a household full of children. Silence!

As a teenager, I made it my job to keep my siblings safe. And to do that, I had to keep them out of my dad's way – when he was angry.

I also made it my job to help my mother as much as I could. So many kids and only one mom.

After baby number eight, she became depressed with what I believe now to have been post-partum depression. To this day society struggles with accepting and treating depression of any kind, but back in the '60s, there were truly minimal resources for my mother. Because of the lack of resources and probably feeling very alone she eventually attempted suicide.

The day it happened I knew something was wrong. She was distant and would not talk to anyone. She literally did not speak a word. I followed her all morning trying to figure out how to help her. Finally, she spoke – she said "Connie, go out and play". I did not want to, but I left the house to play outside with friends.

If I would have stayed in the house, I might have been able to see her take the knife downstairs and intervene. I could have prevented this horrible event that happened in our family. This tore me up inside and it took a lot of years to not distrust my gut feelings.

That day was also my first remembered metaphysical experience.

Luckily, my father found my mother downstairs in the basement and was able to stop the attempt. As soon as the ambulance left with my mother, I went back into the house to replay the scenario. I was so mad at myself and so curious to see what I could have done differently.

I went to the doorway between the living room and kitchen where if I had stayed inside, I could have seen my mother take the knife. At that moment, a large ball of energy went down my body from far above my head, down to my feet.

I heard a voice say, "DO NOT BLAME YOURSELF!". The voice was immensely powerful! I had to listen to it. I was not, under any circumstances, to blame myself. However, that is easier to do in spirit than in reality.

While my mother was hospitalized, my dad still had to go to work so the children that were not in school stayed with the many Aunts and Uncles we had and who wanted to help. United Way provided a nanny and we trudged on.

Every lunch period I would find a place on the playground to remember where the children were. Since they were scattered around to different family members at different times, I wanted to make sure I knew where each one was that day. I would hold up four fingers and name the sibling and the family they were with. It was so important at that time to have some sense of trust. Of knowing they were safe.

I think I became even more hypervigilant and purposefully more energetically small. Everything I did was because of some external cue. Take care of the kids so mom can relax and be happy. Take care of the kids so they do not upset dad and get hit. Be small and stay safe.

This was a time, for me and I think most of my brothers and sisters, of walking on eggshells. We did not understand what fully happened to our mother, we did understand that dad was stressed.

Probably the hardest part was being told by our father, under no circumstance, were we to cry when we could visit our mother in the hospital. This was extremely hard, as you can imagine. To not feel your feelings. Luckily I had my hiding places where I could cry.

At some point, we were able to get our mom back. With some help, she returned to being her loving, kind, self. We could finally return to doing some of the more normal activities that a family of eight could do. One of those activities was my personal favorite, going to the library!

THE LIBRARY

I have loved going to the library for as long as I could remember. A place where I could learn anything my heart desired. Could anything beat that? Play with dolls? Play hide-n-seek? Nope. Give me the library any day.

I can remember being 4 years old and standing behind the driver's seat (this was before seatbelts) and fiercely watching for when the library would come into view. I literally would start jumping for joy.

When I was closer to 6, I would simply peruse the card catalog, see what interested me, what new thing I wanted to learn, and simply go get the books. I could take up to 5 books home. How marvelous is that?

This is where my curiosity could soar!

It was CURIOSITY, that special essential quality, that helped me to heal.

My mother supported my curiosity by reading to me, inspiring me to read and learn as much as I could.

My father loved trying new experiences.

The time was the early 60's and my dad would take us to experience different churches and different types of spiritual services. My favorite was being in a church, sitting up near the altar. People playing guitars and singing funky songs wearing bell-bottoms and flower headbands. Even then it was more my style than sitting in a hard pew, sit, stand, kneel, sit, stand, kneel.

Our dad would take us to the planetarium and museums. We got to see King Tut's tomb in Chicago, go to the beaches of Lake Michigan, and take vacations to various states (in a very crowded station wagon).

My curiosity only grew through all these experiences and provided me the foundation and knowledge I would need to begin my journey from camouflage chameleon to the Well-Being Warrior.

When I turned 16, I began observing my life and thinking about what I wanted out of life. I came to this conclusion:

All I wanted was to feel at peace, in my body, in my soul.

Shortly after that revelation, I came home from the library with a book that would set a direction for me and for one of my life's purposes. It was a book on yoga. In the introduction it talked about how being flexible and strong in the body can also help the mind be flexible and strong. I knew I wanted that – I wanted an open mind. I wanted to know more about this body/mind connection. I wanted to feel peace and trust, strength and openness in my body and my mind. To replace it with what I knew was mistrust and anxiety.

How my insatiable curiosity brought me out.

How to reconcile a sense of fear and mistrust of myself and the world, trying to remain small and unseen… and an insatiable curiosity of the world?!

Well, how about I read just about every self-help book out there.

Somewhat helpful.

Even in graduate school, I had such fear of speaking up and raising my hand to ask a question, but I did it anyway. My curiosity would trump my fear.

What really helped me was meeting my husband, falling in love, and realizing that, of course, I wanted children. I did not know what my future would look like, but I did know that I was going to raise my children differently than the way I was raised. To do that, I needed help.

I was in it for the long haul and decided to do some major therapy.

I will always be grateful to our two children, Kurt and Alexis. Because of you two, I started becoming a better version of myself. You two bring such joy to me, to us, and you continue to teach me along the way.

I also joined a women's spirituality group. The teacher, also my therapist, ran a three-month group for women wanting to expand their spiritual life and work on their psychological issues.

Over 20 years later, that group still exists. I am thinking that as long as I'm breathing, I can continue to grow - my essence.

As we all know, it can be extremely uncomfortable to choose to look within oneself. The grief, shame, etc. that can come up is amazingly hard to look at.

THE WARRIOR EMERGES

Because of my curiosity to understand myself, and really the human experience, I was and am, able to continue to look at the barriers to knowing my essential self.

I now lead yoga classes, am a leader in a local toastmaster's club, have my own acupuncture practice and continue to feed my entrepreneurial spirit, my curious spirit.

I have a wonderful relationship with my children, my daughter-in-law, my granddaughters.

To this day, my sisters and brothers are close (not that we do not have drama now and then) and we truly know that we all have each other's backs, no matter what.

I am so thankful for my husband for his support. My heart feels overwhelmed as I wrote that. "Thank you" is extremely understated.

I don't believe I would have such a wonderful life if I stayed invisible.

Oh, and I AM a Ninja. I have studied various martial arts for over 12 years. Ninjitsu was my favorite. But now, I am not a Camouflage Ninja but a ninja warrior at connecting to my essence and helping others do the same.

ACKNOWLEDGMENTS

I would like to thank my husband, children, daughter-in-law, and my siblings for helping me be the best version of myself. And since I won't stop facing the barriers to my full potential you're all in it for the long haul with me. I'm so very grateful you are all in my life.

ABOUT AUTHOR

Connie lives in Colorado where she loves to bike, hike, walk her dog and enjoy the mountains. She loves teaching yoga and will hopefully forever be able to get on the ground to play with her grandchildren.

ABOUT MY BUSINESS

Connie teaches mindful, kindful yoga. Always reminding everyone to be compassionate toward themselves and know they have their own inner wisdom to always draw from. She is also the creator of Stress-Relief in a Box®. Because we can all use some extra tools to deal with stressful times.

Website
www.ConnieWarden.com

Facebook Personal Page
https://www.facebook.com/connie.warden.3/

Instagram
@ConnieWarden

THANK YOU OFFER

Free Strategy session,
Connect with Connie for a free personalized yoga class.

Angela Witczak

BECOMING EPIC

The very definition of epic is to be particularly impressive or remarkable, also grand in scale or character. I never realized how epic my life was, until I took a look back and understood that the beginning of any epic life starts with just one step.

When I was 35 years old, I was diagnosed with Multiple Sclerosis (MS). It is a chronic autoimmune disease that affects the brain and spinal cord, causing symptoms such as numbness, impairment of speech, fatigue, and blurred vision, as well as a variety of other symptoms, each unique to the person who has the disease.

I had just given birth to my son Eli, and I was spending a lot of time in the gym. The gym that I belonged to was amid a program to shed twenty pounds in six weeks. Naturally, I wanted to get rid of that extra baby fat from the last 16 years of carrying children, so I was all in.

I was going to the gym five days a week. I was kickboxing, lifting weights, and doing cardio. I even learned how to hula hoop at 35 years old. Then one day, when I was in the middle of a lifting set, my fingers felt a little numb. I did not say anything to my trainer because I thought I must have pulled something, so I pressed on.

I had been a personal trainer for a few years before my last pregnancy. I knew about proper form, technique, rest, and all those things that you should do to keep yourself healthy. However, I also had a goal in mind about what I wanted. I just kept showing up to the gym. I was not going to let a few numb fingers and toes stop me from reaching my goals.

By the end of the next week, my legs, up to my waist, and both of my arms were experiencing extreme numbness. I called my doctor, and they ran a lot of tests. Their concern was whether or not I had a stroke at 35 years old, after my son's birth. Apparently, that is a common thing for women who have "geriatric pregnancies."

They poked me with a sharp pin up and down my legs. "Can you feel this? Can you feel this? How about here?" Up and down, they poked me several times during several appointments. They told me there wasn't anything to worry about unless the numbness moved up past my waist. If that were to happen, then I should go straight to the emergency room. I didn't feel reassured that I should not worry. In fact, I was very concerned.

Within a week, I was in the emergency room as the numbness and tingling had spread. That's when the doctors decided I should have an MRI done. 2 hours on my back in a tiny little machine, with all the whirring, dinging, clicking, and popping. If you have ever had an MRI, you know what I mean when I say it takes claustrophobia to a whole new level. If you have never had one, well, let's just say that I don't recommend them.

My insurance would only pay for an initial MRI, so when my test results came back, I was recommended to see a specialist. We drove an hour to the University hospital where the doctor we were seeing specialized in neurology and, more specifically, Multiple Sclerosis.

I didn't need a doctor to tell me what I was experiencing. By then, I already knew. I have an aunt and an uncle (who has now passed on) that have the disease. I saw my aunt go through many stages of it, to now, where she has to sit in either a wheelchair or push a rolling walker. Her brother, my uncle, by the end of his life, his speech was unrecognizable; he wheeled himself around in a motorized power chair and lost a leg due to complications between diabetes and MS.

I knew what I was facing.

It had been over 40 days since I had a normal feeling in my arms and legs. I wasn't even sure if I would ever regain feeling again. I knew many women that had that sense of tingling in their limbs that never went away.

That day, the doctor informed me that I had some lesions on my spinal cord and that to know if I actually had a diagnosis of MS, I would have to have another MRI, this time with a dye added to see if there were any enhanced lesions on my brain or spinal cord.

That MRI took close to three and a half hours. Three and a half hours of me not moving, laying still, on my back, which was causing me excruciating pain. A nurse gave me some valium before I went into the machine, and I can't say that it helped. What I do know is, it was the most prolonged three hours of my life, and I just kept saying to myself, you can make it another 5 minutes. Then I would count to 100. Over and over and over. When that stopped working, I started thinking, and dreaming, and doing everything I could except worry about the outcome. I spent each moment grateful to be alive and knew the MRI would eventually be over.

I got a call from the nurse about a week later. She wanted to tell me the results of my MRI but did not want me to worry.

"Its Multiple Sclerosis."

I had already guessed that. What I wanted to know was what I was going to do next. I was given a variety of different treatment options, the biggest issue was that I was breastfeeding Eli, and I would need to stop.

I had never had the opportunity to breastfeed any of my children before. He was my last child, and I wanted every moment I could spend with him, including breastfeeding. I told my doctor that the treatment would have to wait.

I was informed that the lesions could continue to grow and that my symptoms would worsen if I didn't start right away. I read all the packets of information given to me, and I knew that the medication was not a cure, so I was willing to take my time with Eli.

I eventually regained feeling in my body but experienced a daily struggle going through the flare-ups. There was a point when even walking from the couch to the bathroom was exhausting to me. One time I even got up off the couch, and the next thing I knew, I was on the floor with a twisted ankle because my legs had gone numb without me realizing it.

I spent almost two years that way, not working, just doing the "mom thing" while I chose Eli over my health. But I was getting worse, and everyone knew it. My doctor requested another MRI. 3 more hours in the tank of claustrophobia. Afterward, Eli and my husband brought me flowers. A few days later, the doctor called and told me to make an appointment.

My lesions were worse. I had more. More on my brain. More on my spine. 12 to be exact. I needed to consider treatment immediately. And so, I did. I started on a drug that involved me giving myself daily injections.

Every single day I needed to put a needle up to my body and put these drugs into me. I did not think I could do it at first. In fact, for the first two months, I made my husband do inject me while I would look away from the needle. And then one day, I just sucked it up and did it. I spent several months covered in welts until I could figure out the right thickness to shoot my subcutaneous fat. It wasn't easy. But I finally figure it out.

Eventually, the numbness stopped altogether. I had spent a good two years wallowing in this disease. Now it was time for me to do something epic. Now it was time for me to take action.

A HALF MARATHON

It was time for me to get my life back. And so, I went for a walk. I made it three blocks from my house before I had to turn around and walk back. The six blocks that I walked took me 17 minutes. Before my diagnosis, I could walk a mile and a half in that amount of time. It was not what I would call epic by any means, but it was epic for me, right then.

That was the most significant, grandest thing I could do in my life at that moment. And then, I walked some more. I walked for a few weeks, and then it turned into a few months.

Then, I decided to sign up for a running challenge. I had been in a "runners group" online for several years before I ever got my diagnosis. On the first of October that year, many of them were starting a 50 5k challenge. That meant that every single day they were going to run a 5k for 50 days in a row. The farthest I had walked at that time was maybe 2 miles. A 5k is 3.1 miles.

I knew it was a little crazy, but I signed up. I put my mind to it and said to myself, I am doing this. I knew that I was not going to be able to run. I could barely make my legs regularly work, in any sort of consistency. But I was going to do this. I had to do it.

The first day I set out with Eli in his stroller. He doubled as my walking buddy and a walking stabilizer. I walked and walked and walked. Who knew that a 5k was SO far. It felt like a marathon. It took me an hour and 15 minutes to get done. I was not going to break any records with my 5k time, but I got it done.

Each day, I got up with the mindset that I was going to do it! No matter how I was feeling, I was going to get after this goal. It was not easy. There were days that it rained, and I felt like quitting. But each day, I got up, I put my workout clothes on, and I went for it.

Near the end of my challenge, there was a local race in my town. It was a 10k run for charity. The race was twice as far as the distance I had been going. I ran the course twice before race day and believed that I would be able to do it. One of my friends signed up with me, and we chose to do it together.

Now, when I say I ran the course, I am really more of a "wogger" which is the cross between a jogger and a walker, but it was still something. I knew I would never break records, but that was not my goal. My goal was just to be a part of it and finish.

Race day came, and Jenny(my friend), Eli, and I started on the course. It was tough. When we came up the final hill to cross the finish line, I was so excited. I had done something huge! I not only completed my 50 5ks in 50 days, but I also did a 10k!

We came in dead last. So far last, that the organizers had taken down the finish line, the timer, and were handing out the awards to the finishers. I did not care because dead last still beats, did not start!

Talk about epic. At that moment, I felt I had done something epic! I might not be a world record holder of the fastest mile, a star basketball player, or even some movie star, but at that moment, I felt like I was a queen of the entire world.

I did not stop there, though, because I wanted more! I wanted to truly see how far I could go to beat this disease. When you have an autoimmune disease without a cure, there are only two things that you can do. You can face your day with disappointment, or you can get on with your life and live your best life ever. That is what I wanted to choose for myself.

Not long after, I found a race designed for all women of any shape, size, or ability to do a half marathon. I was intrigued. 13.1 miles is an exceptionally long way. It is especially far for someone who doesn't have control of her legs at any given moment.

But I wanted to try. I wanted to prove to myself that I could do anything. Naturally, I did what any good and slightly crazy woman would do; I wrote an impassioned letter to the creator of the race applying to be a race day ambassador. I told them of my struggles with MS, and I wanted to be chosen as a face of the race for every woman. A race where women can do anything.

I did not think I would get chosen to be one of the ambassadors, but I was! And that meant that I would have to DO the race. I started very slowly training and practicing to "wog" 13 miles. I was so slow. There were days I was sure that I saw a few turtles pass me on my journey, but I continued anyway.

The time came for me to show up on race day to prove to the world, and myself, that I could do something of this magnitude—a half marathon.

I got up that morning with great anticipation, and then the fear started. Every what-if that I ever carried around was weighing me down. I had looked at the weather report and found out it was going to be incredibly hot. I had not been training nor preparing for the heat that happened that day.

And then, I thought to myself; this is no big deal. If I can be the mother of 8 children, I can do anything. The starting buzzer went off, and I started on my journey through the streets of Madison, Wi. The first couple of miles were comfortable, and I kept on smiling for all the candid photographers that were on the course. Somewhere mid-way through the race, though, I began to lose feeling in my legs. I didn't have Eli in the stroller with me or any way to keep myself stable, and I just needed to press on.

Around mile 6, a woman caught up with me, and we began to walk/run through the streets together. By mile 9, I was ready to give up.

At some point in the race, I needed to stop because I hit a wall, both physically and internally. I started telling myself how stupid I was for even thinking that I could do something as incredible as this. And then, several women stopped to offer assistance. One offered to go the next mile with us. One offered me a power bar. These women rallied around me so I could keep going to the next step.

By mile 11, though, my body started telling me that it was time to be done. I was going slower and slower, and by this time, I had lost all feeling in my legs and arms. I was not sure how I could even go on any longer. But step by step, I did go on, with all the strength I could muster.

One mile before the finish line, a couple of my friends, who were actual competitive runners, came flying past me. They had a later start time than me, so essentially, they were lapping me. As they checked in on me, I knew that I was fading very quickly and that I would need medical attention by the time I crossed the finish line.

They promised to run ahead and have someone ready to help me.

With dedication and perseverance, I crossed the finish line. The woman that joined up with me at mile 6 had to hold my arm up in the air so that I could high-five the people standing along the finish line. The medics met me on the other side of the line and carried me to the medic tent.

A CROSS COUNTRY RUN

I tried to pretend that I was fine, and after 10 minutes or so, I got up and walked into the air-conditioned building nearby. I promptly collapsed in the hallway, where I was not okay. I was overheated and dehydrated.

I earned myself a ride by ambulance to the nearest hospital. Someone called my husband to meet me, and the rest is a blur. I am told they packed me in ice and pumped me full of medications and fluids. I felt foolish that I needed my husband to rescue me on my epic journey to prove that I could beat this disease.

As a safety net, he was there to pick me up. It made me remember that even the best athletes fall sometimes, and they just pick themselves back up and do it again. They not only do it again, but they also go for longer races, better times, and something even more epic than the one they tried before.

After my epic failure of ending up in the hospital, a woman had reached out to me about what I had accomplished while having MS. She had told me that there was a run that was happening the following year. A cross-country run. It was a relay to raise money and awareness for people with MS. Most of the runners were cross country runners that participated in events like the Ironman, or weekly marathons. And occasionally, they would have someone with MS sign up.

I wanted to do it.

I wanted to be a part of this cross-country run. So, again, I sent my passionate letter to the coordinator who interviewed me for one of the spots. "I am not a runner," I told her. "I can barely run a 15 minute mile, and I collapsed the last time I did a half marathon. You should choose me because I want to prove that I CAN do this."

I got the invitation in the mail a few weeks later. Then, I had to tell my husband what I had done. He thought I was slightly insane, and yet he was supportive. We quickly worked out the logistics as to how he would manage me being gone for 12 days, and then I got to work. I met up with someone who could run circles around me, and every day we met for our "run."

I was slower than molasses in January on a cold Wisconsin day, but I was out there doing it. I was not getting any faster, I was stayed consistently slow and steady. My body also seemed to understand that this getting up and going for several miles a day run was the new normal. I was no longer losing feeling in my legs and arms daily, which was a good sign.

The training was brutal. There was a time that I considered quitting, but I didn't have it in me. I knew that this was something that I had to do.

After speaking with the coordinator of the race and planning the route that would best serve me and not kill me in the process, the plan was for me to run 100 miles across the state of Colorado in 7 days.

The first morning we started early to beat the sun, and I genuinely thought I was insane the entire time. I was hot, my body was exhausted from all the training, and the roads were flat. Again, I had not prepared for this.

I do not know what I was thinking about signing up for a cross country run when some days I could barely walk. I was only able to go 12 miles the first day. I could see the disappointment in the SAG crew's eyes. I was not their typical marathon runner. In fact, I was nothing like the rest of the team at all. Usually, the rest of my teammates went out and ran their marathon in a few hours and then had the rest of the day off. It took me over three hours to finish the first 12 miles.

We went back to the camper where we were staying, and I showered and sulked. I knew that I would need to pick myself up out of this destructive way of thinking and put my mind to work. I told myself daily that I could do anything.

The days were hot and incredibly long. The weather was in the mid-'90s, and there was extraordinarily little shade on the road that I was running. By day 4, I was sunburned, had excruciating pain in my legs, and missing my family. I knew that giving up wasn't an option, and I could have asked one of the SAG team members to take a few miles for me. I was unwilling to waver. I had to keep trying to conquer the great unknown of this disease, and I was planning on winning the battle.

On the morning of day five, I still had 46 miles to go over the next three days. I was going to have to push through. But the first step I took that day, I knew something was wrong. My knee was killing me. The first SAG stop was at mile 4, and it took me way too long to get there. I took some ibuprofen and kept going.

My knee was swollen, and every step I took felt like razors slicing me through my legs. Tears were rolling down my face by the time I made it to the 8-mile mark. I didn't think that I could go any further, but the SAG team encouraged me to press on. I had too many miles that still needed to be covered, and it was getting hot out. It took me almost two hours to finish those last four miles to make it to 12 miles. I needed to stop.

There was no way I could keep going with the pain that I was experiencing. We drove back to the camper, and I showered and stretched out. The talk was that later that evening, I would go out and do four more miles so that I could have fewer miles over the last two days. I decided that I would wear my favorite sandals instead of running shoes. I would give my legs a break with a different pair of shoes.

My sandals felt great! In fact, my knee pain was gone wearing my sandals. I couldn't explain it, but I was feeling so much better. I even started running. Actual running! When I showed up at the SAG stop faster than they expected, my team was surprised when I told them that I wanted to keep going!

I ended up going 20 miles that day. The farthest I had ever gone in a single day. All that was left was for me to accomplish was one marathon. And I still had two days left.

The next morning, I got up, and I set out in my tennis shoes. We brought my sandals along just in case, but I had wanted to at least start in my shoes designed for running. After the first 4 miles, I changed my shoes, and I made the decision, I was going to finish this in one day. I wanted to have a marathon under my belt.

At that point in my life, the most challenging thing

that I had ever done was given a child up for adoption when I was 20 years old. This feat felt even more challenging than that, at the moment. I just kept walking. I kept putting one foot in front of the other, without stopping. I ignored the pain in my legs and just kept going.

We stopped for lunch and a small break, and then I told the team I would finish the relay that afternoon. My support team said to me that I could only go until dark, and for safety reasons, they would have to pull me off the road after that. Everything in me wanted to finish that day. I had wanted to get up early the next day and drive the 14 hours home and surprise my husband.

That afternoon, I went back out to finish what I had started. That evening I could see the darkness was setting in and the SAG vehicle up ahead waiting for me. When I got there, the team said, "You have one mile left. You can do it now, or first thing in the morning." I knew without a shadow of a doubt I was going to do it right then.

I cried for the entire last mile. I had "Fight Song" playing on my radio, and the words were playing through me with every step I took. "This is my fight song, take back my life song, prove I'm alright song…and I don't really care if nobody else believes, cause I've still got a lot of fight left in me."

I crossed the finish line and laid down on the ground, and sobbed like a baby. I had done it. I had done a marathon with Multiple Sclerosis. I still had the feeling in my legs; I was not headed off to the hospital. I felt great. It was then that I realized how genuinely epic I was. That I was able to accomplish anything I set my mind to do.

A RENEWED SPIRIT

I had done the impossible. Except, it was possible. It gave me great strength and mindset that whatever I set out to do, I could do. No matter what.

I came home from that epic journey changed and with a renewed spirit. I decided on the long drive from Colorado to Wisconsin, while I cried and laughed about what I had accomplished, that I was no longer going to carry the weight and the burden of being a patient of MS.

Since coming home, I found alternative treatments that I take for myself, and I no longer take daily medication for my symptoms. I stopped claiming I have this disease that holds me back. I treat myself to living my best life, and carrying on with the CAN-DO attitude, and I continue to believe that I can create and accomplish epic things if I just put my mind to it.

My journey across Colorado was over three years ago, and I am still in awe of what I could accomplish. I no longer have a desire to run everywhere. In fact, I realized after my epic journey that I don't even like running! I still walk a 5k almost every day, though, to remind myself of how far I have come.

I live my life now, knowing that there isn't anything in this world that can hold me back. I wake up with purpose and passion that fuels me each day. I know that I am bigger than some diagnoses. I bought a company that I love, and I spend my days serving customers that bring me great joy. I serve on several non-profit boards, working to change the world. And I run circles around my family members, knowing that we only have one life to live, so we have the opportunity to fill it with greatness, every day.

Whatever you face today, whatever your challenges are, you can do it. You can live your best life. Sometimes that means going "all in" and going after the truly epic things. And sometimes epic merely means going for a walk that is just three blocks long.

Everyone that ever did anything tremendous and epic in their life did not start out doing epic things. No, they started small and built up to it, one step at a time, one business deal at a time, just one thing at a time. Like I have done, and so many others who have gone before me.

Just like you can do. You can start now. You can start today. On this epic journey, we call life and go after your dreams. You can say to yourself, one day, someday, or day one starts today.

I love you. I believe in. You can do it!

ACKNOWLEDGEMENTS

Thank you to my amazing husband, Edward, for always being my cheerleader, no matter how crazy my ideas are. I love you.

ABOUT AUTHOR

Angela Witczak is a wife to Edward, and the mother of eight children. She currently resides in Baraboo, WI where she is an author, speaker and entrepreneur. She is passionate about helping women to find their purpose and belonging in life, and reminding them that they are loved.

ABOUT MY BUSINESS

Angela's purpose is to help women to be the very best version of themselves, spiritually, physically, mentally and emotionally. She helps to move women through the chaos in their life, to help them find peace, love and joy through her coaching and through her written word.

Website
choosetoday366@gmail.com

Facebook Personal Page
https://www.facebook.com/angela.mcmurray.18

Instagram
https://www.instagram.com/author.angela.witczak/

THANK YOU

Free Strategy session,
Please reach out via email or on my website for a 30 minute call discovery call to find out how

Nicole Majik

A LIFE PERCEIVED IS A LIFE RECEIVED – EMBRACE YOUR BECOMING

Where does your story begin? Where do any of our stories begin? They begin with our own perceptions of who we are…during a time when we have no clue who that person is and vulnerably rely on those around us to give us the signals of who that may be.

Growing up I was told a lot of things. I was told:

You can't
You're not worthy
You're not smart enough
Your voice doesn't matter
You will not be accepted for who you are
You're a freak
Sit down, shut up
You're fat
You're ugly
You're lazy
You're an embarrassment to this family
You don't have talent
You don't matter

I may not have been told all of these things in those exact words, but those were the words I heard based on what was said and actions used by those who supposedly love me.

I'm no different than anyone else and no one else is different from me when we break it down to the true essence of who we are: Energy. Love.

Today I forgive. I forgive those people who said the things they said, did the things they did, but most of all I forgive myself for giving away my power and allowing myself to believe these ridiculous things.

Throughout my childhood, I yearned to understand so many things yet felt so powerless against the vast array of forces that seemed to be plotted against me. I grew up a very psychic child in what I considered a radically Christian household. All of my life I could see auras, sense energy and speak to spirits. I saw things that most people couldn't see because they were too closed off or in denial that these things even existed. This was my reality, my world… a world I was supposed to pretend did not exist. I wondered why I was even here if I had to deny the existence of my truth when my abilities that should have been considered gifts were demonic in the eyes of "those who loved me". I often wondered who these people are and most of all who am I? I struggled to be normal when nothing in my life has ever been normal.

I was born on April 15, 1975, at 8:34 AM. A "tax day baby" born to a CPA and a nurse. We often laughed that I was the cause of a lot of extensions that year. I ended up with two sisters and I am the middle child. My zodiac sign is Aries with a Gemini Rising and Gemini Moon. My birthstone is a diamond; my flower is the sweet pea and I am part of Generation X. I am a Tuesday child, full of grace. What does all that mean? Nothing to a newborn baby, but may have meaning throughout one's life, which may prove to be useful…or not.

    Throughout elementary school and into high school, I was put into advanced placement educational programs for "gifted children". These were programs based on various IQ and other types of testing that were performed and the top students were enrolled into programs designed to test our abilities in educational, social, and whatever pilot programs they came up with next. We were brought together once a week to do various training, testing, and tasks. In first grade, a small group of us were bussed over to the high school and were taught programs using Apple computers (back when the floppy disc was high-end technology). We were taught computer programming and were tested in various skills like math, geometry, and science using computer games. In third grade, the gifted students had a combined class of 2nd and 3rd grade and we shared the class environment and usually had 2 classes going on at once as well as mixed grade learning sessions. I believe this was a social experiment as well as a test on the ability to learn while ignoring potential distractions. In 4th grade, I was put in a different school than most of my friends and then brought back to the school for 5th grade. Could this have been an experiment to see how the separation would affect various youth of different backgrounds, social and educational levels? Possibly, but we were unaware of any agendas at that age and just carried on being children at that time.

This was our normal. In 5th grade, I was part of a Stock Market game with this advanced placement group. We were broken into small groups after being taught what the stock market was all about, given newspapers to look at all the stocks that could be invested in, and had to make mock trades with a certain amount of money that we were told we had to start. The progress of each team was tracked for a certain number of months. At the end, the team who made the most money in the stock market was the winning team. Each night after dinner I would review the stocks in the newspaper to see how my stock picks measured up. I quickly learned that my intuition was useful in choosing ones that would do well and staying away from those that didn't do as well. I also learned that overriding my own gut instincts with instruction from my father on choosing stocks was the most horrible thing I could do. He told me to choose GTech stock because it was going to surge, so I blindly listened to him. He was my Dad and I looked up to him. He was smart and knew everything. Well, he didn't! That was the worst stock picked of the week! The stock dropped significantly, and I was devastated, angry and when I was looking through the paper for the next stock pick and he opened his mouth, I told him he was fired and why. I decided to keep doing what I had been doing all along and pick them myself. I still look back at this program and wonder if people were making bets in the actual stock market off our choices and if this was a test of our intuitive powers.

To this day I wonder so many things about those programs that went on through 7th grade, which was my first year in High School. My town didn't have a middle school so it had 7-12 grades in the high school. I found some old testing results showing that I was in the top 1% of the students tested nationwide. I wondered why my parents didn't push me to accelerate even more in various areas in my life and education. I ponder, but I choose not to enter the rabbit hole on speculating that one.

I do remember looking back on so many of the brain tests they did and I always scored right in the center of the brain; neither right or left. I also remember seeing the tests show a dot on a diagram of a brain representing the analyzed results. The dot could be more to the left or right side as well as towards the frontal or parietal portion of the head. Mine always came out in the very center of the brain. I always thought that made me boring until I realized it only made me much more fascinating. The ability to use both hemispheres of the brain at the same time created balance. The ability to use right-brain creativity with left-brained logic made it easy for me to process information from various angles with incredible speed and accuracy.

How does a highly intelligent child in advanced placement programs begin to believe she is not smart enough, not good enough, not important enough, and is unloved and alone?

In my early years, I was quiet and kept to myself. I liked to play in nature, capturing fireflies, grasshoppers, chasing butterflies, and playing in my fantasy world that I could create at any time. I don't remember feeling alone but I did remember not feeling special and that everything in my life seemed to be plain and boring And nothing good ever happened to me. I always wondered if anything good would ever happen to me. it wasn't something that I could really ever imagine at that age. I excelled at everything I put my mind to yet I got bored very easily. In my teenage years I was friends with everybody yet did not have many close friends and started to feel alone no matter who I was around. I hardly ever felt like I fit in anywhere, yet I fit in everywhere. There always seemed to be a distance between me and everyone else. I was kind, generous, accommodating to those around me to a fault. I became a doormat and I didn't like it.

 I also didn't want people to think I was crazy or a freak because of the psychic gifts I had. I could hear spirits and I would often answer questions in people's heads before they could say anything. I learned very quickly to sit down and shut up because I shouldn't be speaking. I learned to quickly hate my own voice. I found it very easy to study for school by recording myself asking and answering questions so that I could fall asleep studying. Something about assimilating that knowledge in an in-between state made it easier to absorb into my subconscious making it easier for me to learn. Anything I needed to memorize I would record yet I used to sit there cringing at my own voice. I absolutely hated it, hated it, hated it. It took me well into my adulthood to get over that until I actually started speaking publicly on a regular basis and started receiving messages saying, "Oh my God, Nicole, I could listen to your voice all day. You have such a soothing, calming voice." "You are so interesting to listen to."

 Why was I so discarded? Why was I "different"? How was I different? Around the age of seven, I realized that I really was different. One day while we were in church I noticed something very peculiar. The priest today was green when he was always purple. Being the inquisitive child I was, I asked my mom: "Mom, why is Father John all green when he is always purple?" She leaned over and asked me, "You see color around people?" When I said yes, she started to ask me a whole bunch of questions related to this interesting sight. I asked her if she could see colors around people and she told me that she could only see a thin white layer around people if she looked closely. I told her there was so much more than that and that's the moment I realized that not everybody sees things the same way that I do. This was another instance where I quickly learned to keep things to myself or I would be interrogated and also asked to violate other people's privacy for someone's curiosity which I knew in my heart was not right.

As I became more aware of the various gifts that I had which were "not normal", I became a little more withdrawn and intrigued at pushing my limits. I had a yearning to learn as much as I could without having a mentor, without having a role model in the metaphysical realm, and being very isolated by my family. We did not have the internet then. I only had my intuition, my guides, and books that I could read only while I was at the bookstore. As you would guess I spent a lot of time at the mall with my friends. I had one friend who I grew close to who shared an interest in the metaphysical. I felt safe with her knowing about my secret gifts. At the time she was the support that I needed to be able to grow in these gifts. Our friendship deepened as we explored this quantum realm together.

I am often asked about my family and if they have gifts as well. They do, however, we look at them from different perspectives based on our belief systems. Everyone in my family is very intuitive, psychic, prophetic dreamers and vision seers. The difference between them and me is that I did not display the same devotion to the Christian faith as they expected from me, therefore my gifts must be coming from a demonic source. This separation and dualism was very confusing to me. Around the age of ten, I started spontaneously astral projecting. I had no idea what was happening to me. I just knew I had no control until I was out of my body. I could feel the sensation of massive vibration throughout my entire body at the onset as well as a whirring noise in my ears and immediately following what I called the tornado which was a sensation of being sucked out of my body. Once I was out I could go anywhere I wanted to. It was similar to the dreams that I would have of flying around and meeting up with a friend down the street but I was awake instead of sleeping. It brought a sense of freedom and control that I otherwise did not have in my life. It was a way for me to escape as well as explore. I was excited about this new gift and determined to be able to control it so I could do it whenever I wanted instead of whenever it happened to me.

One day this escape turned into a nightmare. I came home from school one day to find my room ransacked. Everything was turned upside down. I had no idea what was happening. My mother and my sister told me to go into the family room that evening. We were having a family meeting. My entire family was there as happens with an intervention. I was told I needed God. I was told I was demonic. I was told that I didn't have enough talent to draw as well as my artwork they held before me and that I must have been channeling demons. All of my cassette tapes were confiscated. I remember my Misfits album entitled Evil Live was thrown across the room and broken and then thrown into the fire as was my Violent Femmes cassette tape Hallowed Ground called blasphemous and satanic. But what they were really looking for in all of that debacle was a book. A book that I had purchased to learn more about astral projection when I finally learned what had been happening to me. I had been talking about the book in a note to a friend who was asking me questions back and forth And I was answering those questions. My mother found the note when she was doing laundry, read it and started the process to try to find this book in my room and along the way discovered my music and art were impure and unacceptable.

 I couldn't understand how my family could be so closed-minded. I felt betrayed, lost, and more alone than any other time in my life. It was if they just wanted me to be who they wanted me to be instead of actually understanding who I am and encouraging me to be my own unique self. It is so confusing to be told how unique you are in one breath as it should be celebrated and then to conform in the next breath because you are too different. Even When I was applying to colleges in my last year in high school, when I said I wanted to become a coroner and asked for help in choosing the right path, I was scoffed at and told that my thoughts of doing that for a career was only a fad and my dream was ignored. Feeling lost and alone again, I chose to go to school for biology and chemistry. I wanted to go to Washington State University where they had a brand-new electron microscope which at the time was super advanced technology and this college was the only one that had this groundbreaking scientific equipment. I was told that was too far away, so I had to choose something else. When another school was dismissed, I decided to choose my school based on the fact that I used to go skiing and the other school which was a Christian college was near where I liked to ski. This school being a Christian college was very accepted by my family.

I found my life becoming more and more unfulfilling the more I did what everyone expected of me instead of what I was drawn to do. I got married in August of 1997, the same year I graduated college. I was 22 years old. I worked four jobs to save money for the wedding to help my parents with the expenses. I had two jobs on campus and two jobs off-campus: Microbiology Lab Assistant, Science Tutor, Cashier, and Pharmacy Technician. I took 18 credits every semester and I believed that you had to work really hard to accomplish anything in life…a belief passed on by my father. I was always pushing myself to my limits. What I didn't realize back then was that those limits were not growth creating limits. They were mental breaking points and walls I was creating with limiting beliefs.

Expectations can and will formulate the way you think about your own self-worth—if you allow them to by believing they are important to fulfill, which they are not.

I was expected to:
Be obedient and proper
Strive for perfection
Get straight A's
Speak when spoken to
Do what I'm told
Not make mistakes
Be someone else

I was expected to fit the mold of what my parents' perception of reality was based on **their** beliefs. I was expected to love God. Which God? THE God or your God? Who exactly is God? What is God? I was expected to love the version of God that they believed in and it was not a thought as to what I believed on my own because whatever it was, it was wrong. My inquiries to the truth about everything in life including religion, spirituality and who we all are, and why we are even here was not in alignment with what they believed to be true. I did not fit that mold of my parents' beliefs, most especially their religious beliefs. My gifts were confusing and constantly challenged those beliefs, therefore they couldn't understand me. They couldn't accept me for who I was. Their beliefs held them back from even trying to, so instead of finding a way to understand, love and support me, because they didn't know how they just didn't. I cannot blame them for their actions or inactions. Their behaviors were a result of their subconscious beliefs and programming and in their reality, they truly believed that they were 100% doing the right thing for me. For that, I love them, and I understand now the reasons why they did what they did and can appreciate them for who they are in love and gratitude.

Each phase of our lives gives us a new chance to delve into a deeper exploration of ourselves. Some of us will take that chance and others will circle around aimlessly like spinning in a whirlpool only to experience the discomfort of the same current, the same pattern over and over again. Those who continue the loop lose sight of the true reason for the phase – to learn who we are, so they repeat the pattern until at some point they become aware enough to realize that they have been in an everlasting cycle of projecting or victimizing themselves rather than exploring the true meaning and opportunity presented from that which they are experiencing. My own self-discovery helped me to understand those around me so much better and at very deep levels. I have realized now that this is the only way to align fully with our truth: Know Thyself. The rest falls right into place. How long it takes you to get there is completely up to you and you will only get there when you are real, raw and ready. We need the negative experiences to push us out of our comfort patterns to look at things from a new standpoint and discover the abilities we have to realign with our purpose.

OF LOVE AND MARRIAGE: THE FIRST COLLAPSE

I had a great big wedding… I think it was everything my mother would have wanted. We were wedded on the swelteringly hot second day of August 1997 in the great big Cathedral of SS Peter & Paul in Providence, RI by

Archbishop Pierce. We had the pipe organ played as well as a harpist. The Icon of Mother Mary happened to be at the church that week, so I worked in a special part of the ceremony to honor the mothers by presenting each other's mother with a gift - a specially anointed rosary from Medjugorje and an offering of roses played before the icon. We had the releasing of the doves after the ceremony. My dress was elaborately decorated with sequins and beads that looked like a fairytale wedding dress. Ten of our closest friends and family made up our incredible wedding party. It was really beautiful, and it all went by so fast.

At the reception, I felt more myself than I had to that point – I danced, laughed, and spoke without inhibition. I was the center of attention and it didn't bother me. No one could tell me what I should do that day because whatever I did was just accepted. And then, that day was gone.

Getting married got me out of the house and "out on my own". But I wasn't on my own, I was with another human being that I vowed to live out all of my days with. Someone to love and take care of and hopefully would love and take care of me in perfect reciprocity. How quickly it became yet another set of expectations to live up to rather than the equal partnership it was meant to be.

Six years and two children into the marriage, I found myself in a whirlwind of the unexpected. My husband was acting strangely. He never seemed to want to spend any time with me anymore. He always closed himself off in the lower level of the house and was always too busy. He spent most of his time alone or with a particular circle of friends. He had no time for me, no time for the kids. His behavior only triggered the beliefs that I am not worthy, not enough, not desirable. It festered and grew just like his irritability and anger towards me grew. I was convinced that he no longer loved me when we were attending a gathering at a friend's house one weekend and as everyone stood in a social circle of conversation, he began to slowly and unknowingly move ever so slightly every few minutes until he was standing in front of me and closing me out of the circle. It was a subconscious limbic response because he didn't want me to be there. When I decided I wanted to go home after this happened to me three times that night, he followed up with telling me that friends were going to take me home and he was going to stay out. My old feelings of abandonment, unworthiness, and loneliness settled right back in to camp out and conjure up ghosts of the past once again. These feelings had a field day with my mind. Was it like that night a couple years ago when he was seduced by another girl and shared a kiss? Was it more? Is this the beginning of the end?

    I was miserable and convinced I was going to be alone and forever unhappy. I had a three-year-old and a baby and didn't even realize I was also battling with postpartum depression. I felt like I was going through life as a zombie – just going through motions: work, home, kids, cook, eat, clean, shop, sleep, rinse, repeat. UGH! But then someone befriended me and made me feel appreciated, special, loved…and I had a short-lived affair thinking my husband was having an affair too and if he was going to hurt me, I may as well do the same back. He was having an affair, only I found out his affair was just not with another woman, his affair was an ever increasing drug habit he had been keeping secret but couldn't be kept secret for much longer. When bills can't be paid because there is no more money to pay them, everything escalates like the heat of the sun through a magnifying glass…and I felt like the poor ant that wandered into the beam. The tension grew. I was working. He was home, disabled. No matter how much I worked, side hustled, and shopped frugally, there was never enough. It got to the point I was having to feed a family of 4 on $60 every two weeks. I couldn't understand what was happening until I found out.

Our secrets were revealed to each other and more turmoil ensued. It was much easier to blame the other for the things we had done rather than actually look within and take the necessary responsibility to learn and grow. But who wants to be humbled when they feel humiliated, right?

THE MIRACULOUS SHIFT

I spiraled into an extremely depressed state of mind. I fantasized about my death incessantly. I was continuously reminded about my children and would talk myself out of taking my own life. This happened at least four to five times every day for months and months on end until one day, something profound and inexplicable to this day happened to me. I still remember it like it was yesterday.

On Friday, March 3, 2006, I was on my way home from work. I had gotten out an hour later than usual. The song Stinkfist by the band Tool was playing on the radio, and I turned up the volume. At some point after exit 15 on the Massachusetts Turnpike, while I was traveling in the high-speed lane, I noticed there was an accident up ahead on the right. There were three or four cars stopped on the side of the highway and another one down in the ditch. I couldn't tell if it was on fire or just smoking. As I approached where the cars were, traffic was slowing down significantly, yet still moving steadily and not really backing up. We were moving at a rate of approximately 40 mph. I glanced over at the vehicles without turning my head but didn't see anything telltale of what happened so I quickly looked back to the road. At that instance, there occurred another accident on the opposite side of the highway. It was then that things made a quantum shift. Everything was going in super slow motion and I was processing and thinking to myself at super speed. All the details came into focus. I looked over and saw a woman driver with dark curly hair bouncing and swaying from side to side from the impact. Her car was severely dented on the driver's side door. I remember asking myself where the car was that hit her and how the heck did that even happen when she was in the high-speed lane on the opposite side of the highway. There was merely one Jersey barrier between us. It was then that I saw a car that went up the barrier and became airborne. It was going to hit my car! It was coming down to land right where I was ... Right at my steering wheel. I could see the male driver's face contorted by his screams. It was as if our eyes met for a fleeting instant. At that moment I realized that the front of the car was going to crash down on my car where the steering wheel is, then topple over, pushing in the roof of my car crushing down on my head and breaking my neck and I was going to be dead. I immediately ducked down and to my right as far and fast as I could while letting out an uncontrolled fearful screech. A mental picture of my children and husband flashed in my mind and I said goodbye to them and accepted that this is it. It is over. A sense of peace came over me and everything went black. At that point, it was as if I was the ball in a pinball machine projected forward at such a rapid rate. It was then that I felt a sense of love like I have never felt before in my entire lifetime. Everything became light again and I came to with a giant gasp for air and immediately said out loud, "Oh my God I almost just died! Oh my God, I should have just been dead! " As I said this last sentence to myself, I looked in my rearview mirror to see what happened, hoping that the person behind me was alright to my surprise I was the last car on the highway dash no cars could be seen to the horizon line. I couldn't believe it. Then I thought, "Oh my God am I dead? How is it rush hour on one of the busiest highways and there are no cars in sight on either side of the highway?!" I felt the need to call my mother and thank her for praying for me today and things got even more unbelievable.

 I called my mother and she answered the phone sounding in near panic, "Oh my God, Nykki, are you OK?! I was just praying for you! I always pray for you in the morning but something told me I needed to pray for you RIGHT NOW, so I did! Are you OK?!" I responded with,

"Mom, am I dead?" to which she replied back, "NO, YOU'RE NOT DEAD! YOU ARE TALKING TO ME ON THE PHONE! WHAT HAPPENED?" I told her what happened, and she stated, "You rode angel wings". I remember telling her, "I definitely rode something…wormhole, angel wings…whatever it was I cannot begin to describe what it was like with words in our language!"

When I got home, my husband thought I was exaggerating or making things up. I didn't care what he thought. The first thing I did when I walked through the door was hug my kids with so much love I couldn't help but cry and hold them with a newfound joy and appreciation of life and that was only the beginning.

Almost immediately I began to have the most intense visions I had ever had. I saw things I haven't ever seen and received confirmation after confirmation that everything I saw was real. Future visions always came through and some are still coming to fruition 15 years later! My abilities became super heightened and the ability to see energy and auras became undoubted and a tool to help others be freed from pain and suffering when they were ready to let it go. I had people tell me that where I would touch them, they had massive pains that just melted away and couldn't explain how I knew exactly where the ailments were. I couldn't explain it, but I knew when someone was ready and when they weren't. These amplified and new metaphysical gifts that I received were the beginning of a whole new exploratory phase of my life; a way to explore what the Universe has to offer. It was the opening of the doorway to find my purpose, discover who

I am and create the life I have always wanted to live.

At first, it was very confusing. I didn't know what to expect at any given time. It was exciting and strange and sometimes frightening being stretched beyond limits I thought I had. I found myself to be much stronger, creative and talented than I gave myself credit for. I started tapping into and trusting in my intuition more than ever. I recognized that I was no longer held back by someone else's rules and I could allow myself permission to explore my gifts, so I did and I haven't stopped since.

THE SECOND COLLAPSE: SURVIVING MERCURY POISONING

When I was working as a chemist I was making six figures, managing a team of five lead chemists working on multiple projects in five different countries, and supporting all the departments in the Pharmaceutical Development Division. My job was demanding and stressful, but I loved it and I always had to be on top of my game. Then the unthinkable happened...my health started to decline. I thought it was stress and ignored it and it just got worse. My cognitive functions declined at an alarming rate. A visit to the doctor turned into a year of testing and receiving "normal" results as I spiraled deeper into ill health. I was terrified I would not recover, and death was imminent. I was passing out, couldn't speak normally and it was hard for me to understand what people were saying. Words just didn't register. I had to figure out what was going on. I was the sole provider for my family of six… my husband was disabled and we had four young children at the time. If something happened to me, my entire family would end up homeless. I realized that my life was now in my own hands and I couldn't rely on anyone else for much longer or I most certainly would be dead.

As I listed all the symptoms I had experienced, I thought of all the times that I was able to help others through my intuition, my ability to see auras and work through the torsion field of quantum physics. I decided to use this ability to help myself. I determined that I had mercury poisoning and when I asked my doctor to test me for it he laughed at me. I ended up seeing a heavy metal specialist who said he could not believe that I was sitting here having a conversation with him with the levels that were in my body… that most people with levels as high as mine were either vegetables or dead. This was not an option for me and I started a long and expensive process for my recovery. On the last leg of my recovery, I was lumped into a layoff at work, creating a whole new round of concerns, fears and obstacles for me to deal with.

- My chance for opportunity and growth in my job was stripped from me
- On various levels, my relationships were damaged or destroyed
- I had to liquidate my retirement assets to pay medical bills and maintain my family's standard of living
- My health was far from healthy and my emotional state was rocky

- I was insecure about what the future held, although I was hopeful.

What did I learn from all of this? In the darkest hour, I came to a lot of realizations. All of these areas of my life had to move forward at the same time. I came up with a strategic formula to ensure all of these come together in the right timing and would keep me moving forward, never back and I did it using the methods, the techniques, and the mindset that I teach today. I don't want this process to take other people as long as it took me. Our lives are short and we should live every moment to its fullest. I've overcome a lot of challenges in my life but I have never let my fears hold me back!

FINDING MYSELF

I had the same night terror for five years. It seemed to come out of nowhere. I had night terrors in the latter teen years and into my young adulthood. They feel so real and every detail remembered. The emotions felt in those dreams are so amplified and full of fear and every time I awoke from them I was screaming and crying uncontrollably. I could hear myself but still couldn't wake. As a lucid dreamer who also finds it easy to astral project, this certainly creates a vivid feeling of extreme helplessness and despair. In this particular night terror that I would have at least 3-4 times a week I was bound at each wrist and ankle. In the beginning, the dream was mostly black and I was unable to see what was happening.

I could only think, feel and hear. Over time bits and pieces of the dream would unfold, little by little, revealing more of its atrociousness. My volition to know and understand this dream was being satisfied with a hellish horror with me on center stage. The more that was revealed, the more horrifying and intense it was.

In the beginning of the dream, it felt like there was something I was in agreement with regarding a kind of ritualistic situation, but then the energy changed like I was tricked and now that I am bound I have no say what happens next. Baphomet appears, or someone dressed as such, between my open legs. Four men are securing my bindings at each of my limbs. I begin to writhe trying to escape screaming, "No! No! No! No! N-N-N-NOOO!" and yet I am never able to break free. Each time, I wake up listening to myself kicking and screaming in a powerless panic.

How did it all change? With great surrender, alignment and trust in myself. I realized the more I held on to what I thought I needed to do, the deeper I would delve into a chaotic life. It all bubbled up in 2018 – 2020 to teach me about shifting and stepping into my own fearless authenticity.

My addict son, Jacob, checked himself into rehab in the fall of 2018. He was supposed to enter into a transitional facility in January of 2019. Right at the time that was to happen, there was a heavy rain with flooding in the facility. They had to shuffle the tenants around and close the availability of the beds that were to be taken up by my son and others. I received a surprise call at 7am on a Sunday morning to come pick him up or they would just drop him off at the train station with all of his belongings in trash bags. You can imagine my shock, disbelief and pure dread of what was to happen next. The thought of having my son back at home was so unsettling it ignites tremors of anxiety, mental paralysis, undying waves of danger and severe reticence.

This always seems to happen. Every time I have many good things going on there seems to be something that sneaks in and tries to derail it. Why? My business was scaling up wonderfully! I had so many great speaking engagements and travel booked for events. I even was destined to speak to over 300 people in the fall…I couldn't believe what was happening. I was totally not ready for this or was I and that's why it was happening?

Coming home only sparked all the traumas once again and I ended up giving Jacob a deadline to leave. He found a place in Boston…for a while. He ended up back on the streets, homeless, panhandling, and traveling between Boston and Providence during the summer. As a mom who really loved her children wholeheartedly, it was so difficult to accept the decisions that he made in his life. This was a kid who was brilliant and wanted to be an engineer when he was younger; a child who would come up with crazy diagrams of levers and pulleys, cogs and ramps that actually worked perfectly. All creations from his magnificent imagination. I wanted my son back and couldn't seem to find a shred of him left in the shell of a meatsuit that was his body. He took what he could from the house and sold it on the streets to get his next fix.

It tore me apart feeling helpless towards my son's situation. I felt debilitated and unable to carry out my daily responsibilities as a mom, wife, and multiple business owner. Something had to give because I couldn't give anymore and I didn't want to lose everything I worked so hard to build even though it felt that everything was beginning to crash down all around me. It was in this dark hour that I realized that there was nothing I could do but to surrender. I thought of all the times that adversity struck me down and yet I always got back up stronger than before. I began to understand what true surrender was. I could no longer hold on to the hopes that I could change his situation. He needed to be the one to do that. I needed to focus on my own life, my own journey. My journey was not his journey, nor his mine. Who was I to determine what was good for him or not? I looked back on my battle for my life from mercury poisoning and realized I wouldn't have changed that horror story I lived through and grew tremendously from even though it was excruciating to go through, and I have permanent damage from it. The struggles I have gone through have changed my life in profound and positive ways. I knew I had to trust in the Universe, trust in myself, and trust that Jake would make the right decisions to get him to a place to overcome this hold that the drugs and alcohol had over him. I had to trust that no matter what (and that is a HUGE anything goes type of no matter what) happens, it was meant to be in order for something positive to be birthed from it. So, I did. I trusted. I trusted with all my heart and soul. I released any control I was trying to have over the situation and surrendered. I gave up any attachments to any desired outcomes, beliefs I had about his situation, judgments, or any other negative thoughts, fears and ideas. I simply let go but didn't give up hope. I basically changed what I believed about the given situation and looked at it in a completely different way, one with potential of greatness, no expectations, and walking in truth and trust.

I would hear from him once in a while but typically every week to two weeks to let me know he was still alive, but usually hungry. Then I didn't hear from him at all for months. It was now getting on in the year; fall was turning into winter and holidays were coming upon us. I would leave the window by my bed cracked open just enough so I could feel the cold air and it would wake me shivering in the night. It was a reminder that my son was out there in this cold, it was his choice, to say a prayer of protection over him and to remind me to express my gratitude for having a warm house and cozy bed to sleep in. It was a reminder to have continued trust even though my trust would be tested over and over and, in many ways, some completely unimaginable.

Meanwhile, many other things were all happening at once. Besides my business amplifying and surrendering my son to the Universe, my marriage was quickly coming to an end. In surrendering my son, I also realized that I had surrendered the outcome of my marriage to the Universe several years before and there was nothing else I could do to "make it better". A partnership can never be one-sided. The burdens can't be for one person to bear and the faults cannot be the responsibility of one party. That is not a partnership. I realized that when my husband lost his mother to cancer, the entire family lost him. He spiraled into the abyss of alcoholism and self-isolation and loathing and there was nothing that anyone else could do to "make it better". Believe me, I tried until I was blue in the face yet nothing would work and it only put me out of alignment with my own self. In trying to comfort him, I was losing myself and that wouldn't serve anyone so I pulled back, realigned with my own desires, truth, and purpose, and stayed the course through the storms, rough seas, and tumultuous waves of chaos.

THE ZONE OF FEARLESS AUTHENTICITY

My story is not one of self-pity. It was and will always be a journey of self-awareness, alignment, growth and becoming.

We may never 100% know who we are, but the process of continuously delving deeper into the awareness and understanding of oneself is a necessary process if you want to grow at all. The more I discovered about myself the more aligned I became with my truth, passion and purpose. I understood why I am here to walk this earth and what it means to truly live a fearlessly authentic life devoid of judgments.

All of the obstacles that were in my path were not put there to show me how horrible my life could become. They were there to show me how I can overcome anything and live a life full of love, hope, peace, confidence, and security no matter what was happening in my life. These things only brought out the love I have for my life even more. To some, it sounds dreadful and impossible, but becoming fearless in the face of any adversity has become my superpower that I am now able to share my secret formula with others to do the same. Of all the things that I have "suffered" through in my life, I wouldn't change a thing if it would change where I am now.

Suffering is to tolerate someone or something unpleasant with restraint from interference. We are not meant to suffer. We all have choices we make in favor of ourselves, values, and alignment of our truth and positive beliefs. If we continue to support our negative beliefs, we will never reach our true potential. It is my mission

Helping others to transform their lives from unworthy to unstoppable is the most rewarding thing in existence. That moment after working with my client to permanently erase the self-sabotaging beliefs that derail them and they are faced with a situation that would trigger the negative domino effect and they have the opposite, positive outcome is the best feeling in the world when I get that message of OMG I didn't do that thing! Instead, I did something different and it felt so good!

One of my favorite client messages is this:

*"I never knew how deeply my **past traumas affected me and blocked me** from achieving my life goals. The system **immediately helped me identify** what was rising up emotionally and **showed me how to bring balance**. I now have the **confidence** I was lacking, I understand my **worth and value** and I am **moving forward without fear** toward the goals I have had. I feel **grounded and centered** and I never have felt that way before!"*

Expectations projected upon you are not your

responsibility to fulfill. You are only responsible for following your own true essence and walking in your own divine path. You make the decisions. You create your own beliefs, thoughts, feelings and life.

For the person reading this right now. This was no accident. You are reading these words as a resuscitation of YOUR divine truth, passion, and purpose. You are recognizing your own desires to live a life you deserve without compromising who you are or what you love.

Think about the pains in your life. Why do they exist? Get real and raw and very honest with yourself. Is there the slightest possibility that your perception or the perception of others could have been out of synch and created a meaningless illusion based on beliefs that went against your core?

You are becoming your greatest, most powerful creative self…right now!

Just as I had to go through my own iterations of self-discovery, enlightenment, and transformation, so you are called to do the same. We are ever-evolving and one with the Universe.

Just as I had to realize that all the negative beliefs I had were just lies dimming my inner light, so are you made to shine brightly. Remember:

You can

You are worthy

You are smart enough

Your voice matters and is heard

You are accepted for who you are

You are amazing and unique

You're beautiful just the way you are right now

You have great skills and talents – let them be known
You matter in more ways than you can comprehend
You are loved, infinitely

Always remember these things. Tell yourself daily as a reminder that you can surrender and not give up. You are strong and capable. All the obstacles before you are merely lessons and opportunities put forth so you can grow into your amazing unique self.

I find it interesting how We never 100% truly know what our reality actually is. Our reality is based upon our perceptions of our situations and circumstances. How we interpret any given moment shapes our beliefs. Our beliefs then create the patterns, feelings, and thoughts that we then design our reality with.

A life perceived is a life received. Embrace the possibility that there are countless interpretations in any given situation, and you will find a whole new way to become the creator of your world and master manifester of all you desire.

Choose your beliefs wisely.

Infinite Blessings,
Nicole Majik

ACKNOWLEDGEMENTS

I would like to thank the Universe for all the synchronicities, people and experiences I have crossed paths with in my life. I would not be the person I am today without these things. A great big thank you goes out to my parents for the lessons, opportunities and the love you have given to me all of my life. To my children, I love and honor each of you and your own journeys through life. Jacob, for your ever-loving heart and compassion for the underdog; Damien, for your fearless pursuit of becoming enlightened, being yourself and following your dreams; Andy, for your sense of humor, love of buffalo wings and entrepreneurial spirit; Æona for your sense of individuality, creative self expression and standing up for what you believe in. All of you make me proud to be not just a mom, but your mom. To my ex-husband, Andrew for all the laughs, good times, hard times and lessons through and through. It is wonderful that we can always be friends no matter what. A most grateful thanks goes out to my wonder twin, Diane. We met, bonded and created an everlasting friendship in record time. I will always appreciate everything we have been through together, helped each other through and the love and support that we have for each other. Thank you for always being there for me through the fun, laughs, growing pains and sharing in all the experiences that make up this life. Lastly, I wish to thank my wonderful, supportive, patient, loving partner in all ways, Michael. I appreciate you sharing in all of my experiences without judgments, for believing in me wholeheartedly with pure love, compassion and care and for always being supportive in everything I do. I cherish the unconditional love we share between us. I am so happy and grateful to have so many wonderful people in my life. I can't possibly thank everyone individually for having a role in becoming my fearlessly authentic self, but in lieu of that, here it is: Thank you all for being part of my life, including you, the reader. I hope this inspires you to keep moving forward and attaining your own fearlessly authentic self. Enjoy!

ABOUT AUTHOR

Nicole Majik holds a bachelor's degree in Biology/Chemistry and a Master's in Metaphysics. She is an accomplished leadership and empowerment strategist and educator, and has created a highly effective, life-transforming empowerment program: The Alchemy of Transformation™. She awakens your true potential by erasing limiting beliefs and showing you how to live a life you deserve without compromising who you are or what you love. Nicole has appeared on various radio shows, local TV, as a keynote speaker for international conferences and has even appeared on the Travel Channel for Greatest Mysteries: Smithsonian as well as Beyond the Unknown Season 2 Episode 13. Nicole is a proud Air Force mom and lives in Lincoln, RI with the two youngest of her 4 children.

ABOUT MY BUSINESS

Since 2008, Women leaders and holistic specialists have hired me to help them step into their fearlessly authentic selves and align with their truth, passion and purpose. I help them magnetize their desires by creating a personalized roadmap for successful growth while PERMANENTLY eliminating the sabotaging beliefs that derail them. I show them how to quickly and permanently manifest the balanced life they deserve without compromising who they are or what they love. I combine my experience and expertise in Leadership, Communication, Science, Finance and Metaphysics to bring peace and harmony through a 3 step AIR process for eliminating self-sabotage. My highly effective, life-transforming empowerment system, The Alchemy of Transformation™ awakens your true potential by taking you through a proven process showing you how to live a life you love without compromising who you are or what you love. I don't just give you the tools, I train you how to use the tools. My vision is to have as much positive impact on as many lives as possible everywhere I go. I believe that by erasing sabotaging beliefs we can create a peaceful planet filled with people who know who they are and are nonjudgmental of others therefore creating an unprecedented level of awareness and conscious being. Although I mostly work with adults currently, I have always envisioned myself working with children to achieve fearless authenticity at a young age. I am excited to be wherever the Universe takes me. I love igniting interest, passion and curiosity in people and allowing them to awaken their true potential and divine purpose. My clients say, "The time I have saved through the insight and guidance of this program has changed the way I live my life forever! I used to constantly procrastinate, self-sabotage and feel overwhelmed to the point of paralysis. Now, I get to create my own schedule around what I love to do and taking care of ME first. I feel liberated from the shackles I thought was my life and I am actually LIVING a life I love."

Website
www.MajikLLC.com

Facebook Personal Page
https://www.facebook.com/majikllc

Instagram
https://www.instagram.com/nicole_majik/

THANK YOU!

Want to connect further with me? I would love to hear how my personal story impacted you. Send me an email at Majik@MajikLLC.com with "Your story's impact on me" in the subject line. Love free stuff? Go to the Majik Portal to download the free resources available to help you overcome self-sabotage, gain confidence and align with your truth, passion and purpose: majikllc.vipmembervault.com Wondering if working with me is right for you? Schedule an "Is this right for me" call: https://nicolemajik.as.me/claritycall

Amber Trail

FEAR

Fear. How can four letters make such an impact on our lives? We've all been there. We've all suffered from it. We've all in some way overcome it. Fear comes in so many different forms. Fear of being defeated, fear of being rejected, fear of someone you love, fear of losing someone precious to you and fear of failing.

Growing up, I had a good life. I had two parents, a nice middle-class home to live in, a sister and while both parents worked, we were able to afford a vacation once a year. Yes, it was good on the outside. On the inside, I grew up thinking that parents always fight about money. I grew up feeling like I always had to ask for permission to do anything. I can also tell you that fear was a major part of my life. I lacked confidence. I lacked knowing what the right kind of love was. I pursued relationships with boys in high school that were toxic because they paid attention to me. I felt the only way to be loved was to always do what others told you to do.

Moving on to my twenties, I married young at the age of 23. I had my first son at the age of 24. We built a house that we couldn't afford and soon had a massive pile of debt. We both worked but were living paycheck to paycheck. It took a toll on our marriage. We separated a few times and would always get back together. When I was 27, I had my second son. Three years after that, we separated for good this time. The problem was that I never knew how to love. I was always living under the rule of my mom. Let me be clear. My mom was a phenomenal woman and I to this day love and respect her more than ever.

When my mom was little she grew up with an alcoholic, physically abusive father which created an insecure and fearful mother. She never really knew what love was. So, when my mom had children, she decided she was going to love the crap out of her kids. And she did. Too much sometimes. She became so worried about the choices and decisions that we made that she never let us live.

Upon my final separation with my now ex-husband, I was in the process of receiving my master's degree in Business Administration. Divorce proceedings lasted a lifetime. One month before my divorce was final and I was about halfway through my master's program, my mom was diagnosed with Glioblastoma, brain cancer. Stage four brain cancer to be exact. Our world as we knew it was forever going to be changed. On Mother's Day of 2017, mom was planting flowers outside with my dad. She felt dizzy and passed out. Our dad rushed her to the hospital because he knew deep down, she wasn't fine. A few hours later, my sister and I arrived, and the doctors walked in and told her she either had a spinal infection or another brain tumor. See, many years ago (like 20) our mom was sent to Johns' Hopkins to have a brain tumor removed that was on her brain stem. We were told at the time that the best outcome would be that she was going to be blind or deaf. Turns out, there were other plans for her. She came out as healthy as ever.

On our mom's birthday, May 26th she had some tests done at Johns Hopkins again but this time the biopsy of the tumor turned out to be 5 tumors and this time, they were cancerous. My mom turned 60 that day. Dad was already down there with her, so a friend of the family drove my sister and I down to see her. The plan was to attend chemo and see how it went. When August came around, the good news was that the tumors stopped growing, they didn't shrink but they stopped growing. The doctor had her signed up for one more round of chemo.

JUST LIKE THAT

I'll stop here for a second and ask a question. Have you ever watched someone, like really watched someone, just disappear from this life but still be alive? I have. Watching our mom slowly disappear and become someone we had never met before became so surreal and frightening. Then the moment came in August when she decided she was done. Just like that. She was done. At this point, she stopped walking altogether. She was wheelchair-bound and could barely feed herself. Now, don't forget that at this point, I was still in my master's program, working full-time, a single mom and I just started dating someone. The man I started dating became my safety net. He made me feel safe and the next thing we did was get married at the courthouse. You may be asking me why so quick? Quite frankly, because I wanted my mom to see my wedding, even if it was at the courthouse and I knew I loved him.

In December, we found out I was pregnant with my third child. The days became harder and harder for my mom. After much discussion with my husband, we decided that I would quit my job and start helping more with my mom. My sister was living at home and the burden, yes, I said burden, became too much for her and my dad. I tried to help as much as I could but it's never enough. I have so much guilt built up about how much more I could have helped. But, at the time, I felt that I was doing everything I could.

In early March, we found out the sex of this baby #3. Another boy! Oh boy. By mid-March, I got the call that I needed to come to my parents' house because my mom didn't have long. She took a dive quickly. Even though every single day we didn't know when it would happen or what the day would look like, it's still a shock. So, I quickly went to my parent's house to be by my mom's side. As I got there she was breathing very quickly, and she couldn't really talk. She could still see us, and she held our hands. As the hospice nurse arrived to give her morphine, she looked straight at me and I could see the fear in her eyes. She tried to tell us something. As the nurse administered the morphine, her breathing slowed down and she went into a deep sleep. I never knew what she was trying to say.

We took turns staying up with her during the night

and the next day and the next night. We had to give her the morphine every so many hours. We kept telling her that it was okay for her to pass and that we loved her. But, in my mind, was it really okay for her to pass? I didn't feel like it was. It wasn't fair. Why should I have to lose my mom? I was only 32. She didn't get to see her third grandbaby be born. She didn't get to see my sister get married or have children of her own. She was going to miss all of that and that was not okay with me.

On the third day, a Saturday, I had to go with my husband to pick up my van so that Friday night, I stayed at my house. We got up early and went to pick my van up at the mechanic. I had horrible cell service, so of course, I didn't get "the phone call that would change my life". The first thing that pops up on my phone is text messages, a thread with my sister and aunt. I started to read them, and I saw "I can't believe this, it can't be real". I felt physically ill. As soon as I could, I called my dad and he told me that everyone was asleep and when he went down to her hospital bed in the living room, she was gone. I rushed over to their house, held her slightly warm hand and cried. That body, the shell that housed my mom was all that was left. I'd never heard her voice. I'd never get a hug from her again. I would never get to call her up and ask her what to do. My children would never get to call their Nana again.

After the funeral home took her away, I stepped up and became the big girl. I felt that I had to be the strong one and I had to take care of the arrangements and I had to take care of my sister and dad. Yes, I was very bossy at the funeral home picking out everything. It was my game face because I didn't want anyone to see that inside, I was dying. The night of her funeral, I had to go to Statistics class. I didn't have to, I'm sure my professor would have excused my absence, but I felt I had to. Statistics is not my thing and I knew if I missed one of the 8 classes, I would not pass this class. I also knew that my mama would be super ticked at me if I didn't finish my master's degree. School was hard for me growing up but college; college was my thing. I loved learning and studying for my future. The future where I got to pick what I wanted to be.

WAVE OF RELIEF

A few months after she passed, I felt this wave of relief. Relief? Yes. It felt like I was an actual adult, making my own decisions and handling this adult life on my own terms now. See, when I mentioned that my mom loved us a bit too much, it's because I always told her everything. When she didn't agree with something or gave me disapproval of what I was doing, I felt like crap. I felt like I wasn't in charge of my own life anymore. I felt like I had to have permission to buy a car, buy a house, divorce my husband, get a new job. That sense of relief is when I felt that there was no limit on the possibilities of my life. I felt that I was able to go find my purpose. And I did.

One month when another sign of "fear" crept in, I decided at that moment to turn it into an opportunity. I'm the type of person that needs to be constantly busy and on the go. I found myself in a position where I had to be the one to step up and decide what my next move was. See, I was the HR Director for a small manufacturer of custom commercial furniture. When I started, there were 75 employees. Over the course of eight months, I was worried because we were reducing our workforce tremendously, down to now 40 employees and people were constantly living in fear of "what next".

I finally one day ran out of ideas on how to keep myself busy to earn my salary. This wave of confidence came over me and I walked back the hall to the President's office. Two steps before stepping into his office, my heart started pounding and I literally started to shake. Too late to back out now. I walked in and sat down, probably because I would have fallen over if I didn't sit at that very moment. I told him I needed to speak with him, and I shut the door.

I won't go over every detail of that conversation, but I will tell you this, I walked out of there feeling more empowered than ever. We agreed to reduce my hours to two days a week and the catcher? I was starting my own business and he was going to guide me to get it legal! What?! Yes, at that moment, I decided that I wanted to be an HR consultant for other small businesses who didn't have a need to hire a full-time human resource person. The best part, I could work for myself, create my own hours and set my own price. And that I did.

I began this chapter discussing my mom and the impact her life and her death had on me. The thing is though, my mom was the smartest person I ever knew. She was a brilliant teacher, but, when she'd talk about college and careers back when she was growing up, the options were as follows: secretary, teacher, or nurse. What she really wanted to do was be a doctor. And she totally could have done that, but, she was fearful of what society would think and how they would act if she didn't go with the norm at the time.

If I would have pondered over what to do, if I would have told my family and friends what to do, they would have persuaded me to not give up my full-time steady income and just keep pretending to be busy so I didn't get the axe next. I trusted my gut and knew that I would have many struggles ahead, but I never gave up. I never once said to myself, I can't do this. Today, I am the proud Founder and Consultant at The HR Trail, LLC and I have a vision board and ideas that spit out of my brain faster than I can run. I love every single moment of being a small business entrepreneur.

I wanted to be more than someone's employee. I wanted to be the best wife and mom and working mom. Fear got in the way of a lot of my hopes to start my own business in the past. But, I fully believe that I feared straying from the norm because I didn't want to let my family down or myself down. And I believe that this was the world's way of telling me it wasn't the right time to own my own business yet.

LIFE IS SHORT

The transition from employee to CEO of my own business was exciting and intimidating. Would I fail? How would I make my business and personal life work? How do I keep the momentum of my passion going? You see, those questions are questions that fear presented me with. But enough was enough. Life is short.

When I transitioned from an employee of another company to the CEO of my own company, I relied heavily on networking groups and word of mouth referrals, as well as social media platforms to get this business up and running. When I first started my business, I created my own website and as I grew the company, I redesigned my website based off of research and what my ideal client would be looking for when they came across The HR Trail's website.

The business started out small. Just me with no formal "business training". I had this belief that all business owners had to be "salespeople". In a way, they do but not the way I thought. I pictured a door-to-door salesperson and that was not me. I'm more introverted than extroverted and selling to people scares the living daylights out of me. When I joined a networking group, I quickly realized that it's about building relationships and trust.

I also had the belief that owning a business meant working and having no life to make ends meet. Why did I think that? Because that is what my family instilled in me. They always said, "no, you want to make sure you have a good steady job with great benefits." If that was something you heard again and again, wouldn't it scare you too to step out into this big world and suddenly have fear surrounding you about the unknown? This fear didn't start going away until I met other like-minded women doing the exact same thing I was doing, raising a family and owning a business. They were rocking it.

You see, we are molded into a shape made by our

parents when we are little. We grow up with the same beliefs, fears, and thoughts. When you step outside of that mold, it's scary. Panic attack scary. When you start making connections and surrounding yourself with people you admire and look up to, your world, beliefs, values start shaping into what you want in life.

So, I created a company based on the values that I live by and whom I wanted to work with, not whom I had to work with. After tears, laughter, and stress I designed my company based on my experience and what I wanted out of life. I now have a team, redesigned website and we work nationwide instead of locally. How exciting! I was very picky when I decided to hire my team members. They had to fit into specific criteria and their values had to align with the values of the business. I love my team and the clients I work with, isn't that how it should be?

I overcame the fear that was tied to love, disappointment, failure. When you live in fear all the time, you may not even recognize it but when you live with the idea of pushing yourself to the limits, you suddenly release that fear and you have this new four letter word that appears in your life. Free.

ACKNOWLEDGMENTS

I would like to thank my boys for loving their mom no matter what. They are and will always be my number one fans.

ABOUT AUTHOR

Amber Trail, MBA, SHRM-CP is the Founder and Consultant of The HR Trail, LLC , an International Best-Selling Author, Certified Life Coach and an Executive Coaching Chapter Chair for Powerful Women Today. Amber resides in a beautiful peaceful town in Pennsylvania with her three young boys and husband. She loves to travel because every where she's never been is a new adventure.

ABOUT MY BUSINESS

Amber brings in over a decade of HR experience and has created the perfect blend of business expertise and empathy. Amber decided to reinvent businesses through their people. Empowering employees to do more and be more creates a powerful workforce for each employer who is looking to retain their top talent.

Website
www.thehrtrail.com

Instagram
@thehrtrail

THANK YOU OFFER

Book a free strategy session with Amber!
https://ambertrail.youcanbook.me

Tia Bottum

SILVER LINING LEGACY

I would say my life was challenging before, but today in 2020, looking at the last year and facing the next year feels excruciating. Last summer, I was diagnosed and barely survived my first flare with Ulcerative Colitis. Bedridden for two months, during which I lost 30 pounds, was in agonizing never-ending pain, and couldn't stand for more than 20 seconds at a time, usually just enough time to make it to the toilet every 45 minutes to release the blood that was collecting in my large intestine. I couldn't eat, I would dry heave and had extreme nausea. I knew I was slowly dying from malnutrition and bleeding to death. I had to emerge like a Phoenix from the ashes of my old life into a new world of learning how to walk, eat, and survive. I was very lucky after a month the medication they gave me started to work and I changed my diet. The bleeding stopped after almost 2 and a half months. During that time, my husband was also given military orders to report to Korea for a year unaccompanied without us, which I blatantly ignored because, quite honestly, that was the least of my problems at the time. His report date was for May 2020.

Preparing for my husband to leave for a year in early

2021. It took me a good 6 months to wrap my head around the fact that we were repeatedly denied a change of orders. I accepted this was our life, this is what we are handed. I would say I was about 80% confident everything was going to be fine. I have lived without him before, the kids are older, it isn't a combat deployment, I started making local friends, and my kids are with me and both are accepted into great school programs. I had updated my photography studio to relaunch in January. I had already pictured the year full of my son's dance performances, visiting colleges, competitions, meetings, holidays, and making themed boxes to send to him monthly. I planned each month to give myself something to look forward to. The 20% was fearful and dreadful to think about. It was my sickness and health being unpredictable, not having him here for my daughter's senior year, possibly our 16-year-old 'man' dog dying, not knowing if we could afford traveling to each other at least once during the year, not knowing if he could make it back for her graduation, and my son terrifyingly starting middle school were the top things that weighed on me.

 All the other times he deployed I was consumed with him possibly dying. Scared to miss a phone call, helpless in the thoughts that would run through my head that every time I talked to him, would it be my last? This time, I was more worried about myself dying, a very strange feeling.

 Big events in life are like preparing for a marriage or the birth of your child, only focusing on hope and excitement. You kind of get the gist of what to expect, you make plans, research, and you focus on all the good to come. The 'I can't wait for...' moments. It makes you smile thinking of all the positive possibilities, it fills your body with joy and energy. That is what hope is to me, those exciting thoughts. Unfortunately, we never plan for the feelings of frustration, exhaustion, anger, and the breaking of your heart over and over again by unforeseen events. As a mom, as a wife, as a military spouse, and as a woman I never planned for the grit it would take, the strength I would have to have, or the amount of patience I needed to find, out of nowhere, for the days' nobody speaks of. You know what I am talking about if you have ever experienced any of those life events. Never mind the rollercoaster of a chronic illness on top.

UNPREDICTABLE

Cut to spring 2020. Well, well, well...so you think you have life all figured out, do you? Right out of a movie. Blow after blow, month after month, grief has surrounded us and our families. Every month of 2020, so far, someone has died. My husband's youngest brother, his cousin, my cousin's daughter, and a friend. Let's throw in a pandemic to add a little spice. I won't lie, the pandemic part, at first, was a blessing. A silver lining in a storm so big ripping my 'home' apart. A stop movement was the best unknown to me at the time. His orders were paused. Being forced daily into all-day family time. A reprieve. It gave me hope he may not leave after all. Deep down in my heart, I hoped they would cancel his orders, but my mind was telling me life doesn't work that way. What happened was a postponement for him to leave for his year deployment which solidified that he was going to miss my daughter's graduation. More plans shattered.

A memory of a voice chimed inside my head, remembering a wife of a senior ranking officer who spoke to me a few years back who had dealt with well over 10 deployments in her 20-year marriage, stating something I took to heart.

"It doesn't matter how many times he goes, sometimes it will be ok and sometimes it will be gut-wrenching and hard. You would think the first one was the worst, honestly, it was much harder later when the kids were older." She continued into more details of her life during her worst deployment she endured.

Oh, how I wish she wasn't right!

Dang it, how I wish I didn't think at the time, 'but how could it be harder?' I didn't understand. I was stuck in my point of view and my season of life at the time.

Damned if every time I judge someone, even slightly, I get that 'slammed in the face' like a snowplow on the side of the road going too fast that sprays that slushy, rocky, freezing shit all over you, feeling. My northerners know what I mean. Out of nowhere, with little warning of the scrapping sound on the road, you just brace for impact. Of course, you picked the wrong side of the snow pile to walk on because it seemed easier at the time than trudging through knee-high snow, fearing snow on the ankles trapped by boots would be worse. Path of least resistance doesn't always equal less pain. Maybe it's choosing the surprise quick 'in and out' pain versus long-anticipated annoying pain. Split decisions are so quickly picked, sometimes it works in your favor, other times, not so much.

In June 2020, I was sitting at a 40% confidence level of preparedness for this Korean tour. Everything shifted and lost. All my plans were out the window. The plans to visit colleges with my daughter, taking on new photography clients, traveling to Korea, and having a true social life again with other women, all gone. Everything left is of the unknown variety. Even worse than I could have imagined in my paranoid brain. It would take pages to write all the variables I could dream up, from him being stuck there longer to what happens if either of us gets sick on the other side of the planet. A new terrifying world. Unpredictable. No end dates in sight.

Last night, I found myself weeping silently while cuddling with my husband. Paying attention to every feeling I was having. Storing into memory every curve of his body, the feeling of his skin, the way he breathes, the sound of his heartbeat, the smell of his soap and deodorant, and how my body feels as he squeezes me. I try to bank it in my memory for later when I know I will be in pain and alone. He will be on the other side of the world. Our relationship holding on to memories, hanging on to our history, and surviving on phone calls, letters, countdowns, and, hopefully, video chats. Knowing we will grow in different directions and what we have at this very moment will never be again. This will be our longest separation from the day we met. My chest squeezes and I feel like I am breaking, our marriage is breaking, the world is broken.

The next day, the day before he is scheduled to fly out,

he blasts a song in the living room. We slow dance and I cry. I can't talk. I can hardly breathe. In my head, I yell at myself to be in the moment to see all the love we have but I am overcome with the grief of losing him. How do I do this without him? Anxiety, fear, loss, despair fill my mind. I look at his face, a smile is there with not a care in the world. He is the most 'live in the moment' man I have ever met. He is full of joy and love just to hold me. I am grounded and centered as I look into his eyes. He has so much faith in me to handle this all. Can you imagine if we could see ourselves through others' eyes?

WEATHER THE STORMS

Survival mode. When I reflect on my life so far, survival mode has been my constant way of life with a few breaks in between. The funny thing is I don't feel bad for myself, I just think I have a better understanding of certain things in life from what I have gone through and what I do go through. It reminds me of the story about the trees that have strong roots. If the wind never blew, if it never had to go through hard times, then when a little gust comes through it will be knocked down. But the trees that are faced with tough conditions adapt and dig their roots in deep to keep steady, knowing that life gets hard and to prepare.

My mind goes to 'well, I think my roots are pretty strong now, can the storms give me a break?!' Of course, that is only a brief passing joke in my mind. I think of others and ancestors who have dealt with much worse.

Knowing tomorrow could hold the most horrific scenario, I ground myself in today. What is happening today that gives me the time to even consider worse days? If I have time to worry, then my life isn't so bad. Typically, it means today I am safe. Live in the joy today. See the good that is happening right now. So tonight, I will play a board game with my little family, take a picture, put the kids to bed, and then hold my husband's hand while we watch trash TV for the last time this year.

Storms in spring can come in fast and leave fast, while others roll in slow and stay awhile, either way, my roots are deep and strong. I will weather the storms of my crazy life. Yet still, I sit in my room grasping for positive thoughts, looking for the silver lining, forcing myself to believe there is a bigger purpose, actually believing the world is off-balance because anything bad or good in life will have an equally opposite effect. Thoughts of vacationing after he comes back, getting more one on one time with my daughter before she is off on her own, still doing and planning care packages, and oh my gosh the connections I have made this year through zoom with other women has been a true highlight so far. My 'what ifs' change to; it is just too unpredictable to even come up with any kind of case scenario.

Pretending that it will only be a 2-year stint of a 'shit time' personally, from 2019 to 2021, gives me an end date. Hope. Plus as I write this, it means I am halfway through. Though, reality always brings me back. Life doesn't present itself as 'all bad' or 'all good' for periods of time. It is just time mixed with moments and events that lift you up or crush your soul. Like spring weather. Highly unpredictable. One day cold and wet, the next hot and sunny, and sometimes even all in one day. Ever-changing. If you only focus on the cold days, it will seem to drag on, but if you shift that thinking to 'we are one day closer to sunnier days'…it could feel a little better. I always say "the only constant in life…is that life is ever-changing. Genuinely, it is about finding comfort in the unknown. Hunting for the good.

The pandemic shutdown forced almost everyone to live a life like mine. After months of dealing with my new health and disease, this was a relief to see all the people in society live in a world where something invisible could take you out within weeks. For everyone to be cleaner and more aware of germs. It was, at least for a short time, very calming to me. The world ironically felt safer…for me. A true break from feeling completely alone and misunderstood. Now everyone knew what it was like to be locked at home and forced out of freedom. The freedom to visit people, to have parties and gatherings, to go to museums, and to do normal activities with other people. The difference is, everyone else will get to go back to 'normal' and it will be just a memory for them. Other chronically ill, the elderly, and I will continue in a life trapped in a world we don't fit in.

It crushes my heart when I see others freaking out and acting like it won't end. I wish I could protest, I wish I could be angry and fight for change. I don't get that privilege, I am stuck in my body. I am stuck by people vocally judging me as if I have a choice, that I don't matter, that I live in fear, and fuck my life. I feel bad for them because, one day, they will be in a position where they will feel like they won't matter anymore too. It's truly ironic from my viewpoint. It's like seeing people judge parents when they don't have kids of their own.

Nobody is going to come out of this without sacrifice. The pang of this will be felt for years, from losing someone, financial breakdown, facing themselves mentally, reimagining relationships, and loss of tradition and planned moments. A shift in society is taking place now AS we are living through it and building a new future. We get to decide, we are the ones with the responsibility to make the world a better place.

DEFINING MOMENTS

Here I sit, fall of 2020, attempting to give an update of hope and positivity. Well, in true real-life fashion it is mixed with ups and downs. I'll give you some highlights. The first month was great I felt strong and full, completely capable. I got everything on my to-do list done. The next month I was so depressed, my husband and I were fighting and could not get on the same page. I was sure this was the beginning of the end of our marriage. Do you know how hard it is to argue with someone in a time zone 13 hours ahead of you? Let me tell you it is not fun. I felt more crushed than I did when saying 'see you later' on the day he left. The month after, I created a women's Facebook group, Empowering Time Markers. This helped me find purpose, to keep me occupied. It felt like I was helping others and making the world a better place. Then my beloved dog of 16 years, Monty, passed away. The end-of-life care was exhausting. I was up with him a lot because he would just wander around and only slept if I held him but only for five minutes at a time. Watching him shrink, not be able to eat or drink, and my children's hearts break without being able to give them hope. I lost my way for a bit and my health took a toll after which led to a few weeks of recovery.

As I write this, Covid-19 numbers are going up again, shutdowns are coming. I talked with my daughter last night about how surreal life is right now. We are just going on day by day and I imagine in a few years we will look back at this year and cry. The pain that we are not facing. All the craziness we are surviving. The uncertainty of the world right now. When it is all done, we will cry letting go of all the strength it took to get through.

When facing defining moments you have a choice to roll over and let it define you or stand up and choose to make a difference. Use it as fuel. Stand up in your life. Be the ball of resilience. Get creative. Find out what gives you energy, that is what passion is! A purpose is what makes life worth living. Sure I could lay down and wallow using that I am sick, my husband isn't here, we are in a pandemic, and that life is hard. But after surviving last year and surviving everything in life, this time I have is all a bonus. I have an abundance of love, hope, and gratitude to be able to be here in this moment. It might not be perfect or how I planned, but I am here and I will thrive in the power of what I own. I own my choices, my life, and my heart. My greatest strength is love, my love for others gives me purpose.

I invite you to join my women's group for women,

Empowering Time Markers. I want to see others succeed, I want you to follow your dreams. Become who you are called to do. Mondays I go live with updates and the theme of the month lessons or tools, Tuesdays I post a debate, question, or poll to get your opinions, Wednesdays are reserved for workshop lives from women I interview on Thursdays, Fridays are to spotlight your business or career, Saturday is reserved for workshops, and Sunday is all about self-care. January 2021 theme is Money, coming this spring will be Sales, Marketing, and more. I would love to feature you and get to know you. Connect with me through that group or on my social media under "Tia's Crazy Life" or "TimeMarker Photography". The year 2020 was a shift, be sure to use it to your advantage. Always look for the opportunities around, which is the silver lining.

Looking ahead, my family and I are scheduled to move to Texas when my husband gets back from his deployment. The excitement of moving is always fun to me. Planning huge expansions in my business is on the horizon. I give women the encouragement to fearlessly trust themselves and rise in this lifetime. Showing and teaching women their worth through money coaching and archival portraiture is my passion. Leaving a legacy. My pictures will outlive me, my teachings will outlive me, and my books will outlive me. Filling the world with silver linings. Thank you for taking a peek into the small window of time in my life. I am not done, I have a lot of stories to tell, be sure to follow "Tia's Crazy Life" for all my journey updates and releases.

ACKNOWLEDGEMENTS

To the love of my life, my hero, my husband Steven you have my heart forever. I am blessed to share this life with you, making all our dreams come true. Because of you, I have traveled, I have learned, I have grown. Thank you for stepping up to be the man I needed you to be in my darkest moments and hardest days. To my daughter, my first true love, Camille you give me strength and purpose. My life was changed forever the moment I saw you, I realized how beautiful I was when I saw how gorgeous you were. Thank you for holding my hand, watching Dumb and Dumber a million times, and taking care of me in ways that nobody should ever see another human go through, let alone their mom. You make me proud in ways I never know existed. To my son, my soul match, Carson you surprise me in unexpected ways. Your talent, your heart, and your love have me in awe. My dream for you is to see how I see you, you will change the world if you choose to. You are my sweet boy and I am so proud of the strength you have even when you don't feel it. When you are older and read this, I hope you feel the line of strong people you came from. Thank you for inspiring me to be more in this life than I was settling for. To my amazing friends and family, I am lucky to have you. Thank you for the support as I follow my dreams and passions.

ABOUT AUTHOR

Tia is a proud military spouse for over 13 years. Graduate from Walton High School in New York, NYIP (New York Institute of Photography,) and is a Certified Money Coach through the Sacred Money Archetype program. Ongoing studies at different colleges and programs for photography, event planning, money coaching, child psychology, military life training, and more as she is a lifelong learner. She has two children. Lived in seven states so far and well-traveled from coast to coast. A true leader, volunteerism is a priority for her, she has held many leadership positions. A recipient of the Dr. Mary E. Walker award and many other volunteer recognitions for her service. She is currently writing a book series titled Tia's Crazy Life, these will be autobiographical, self-help, and guides with a concentration on military life, parenting, marriage, and chronic illness. Empowering women to rise in their lives drives them. She aspires to create a ripple effect of positive changes in the world in her life as well as travel the world with her husband. She dreams of an RV lifestyle hitting all 50 states to see all the beauty and capturing it all on her camera. She also loves reality competition shows, has an addiction to crunchy snacks, playing board games with family, and watching comedies.

ABOUT MY BUSINESS

Her specialty is in women's portraiture and teaching self-worth through money coaching via Sacred Money Archetypes. During a complementary Art Direction meeting and a quick survey, she plans a personalized photoshoot. Then a half-day being pampered with hair and makeup, delicious food, modeling, and guided posing to capture the best portraits of your life. A day where everything is catered and specifically for you. Lastly, a photo reveal day to choose your favorite hand matted archival prints from the top printing companies in the USA that will last up to 200 years in a beautiful portfolio box or up to 100 years on display will be presented to choose from. As a certified money coach, she encourages women to charge what they are worth and believe in what they do through exercises, visualizations, worksheets, and archetypes. She designed her business around what she needed as a creative entrepreneur and how to best support other women in business. She would love to help you level up your business and life. Empowering Time Markers is a Facebook group that helps women grow in life and business through networking, teaching, and learning. Weekly interviews, workshops, discussions, self-care tips, and more. She would love to feature you, join today!

Website
www.timemarkerlegacy.com

Facebook Personal Page
https://www.facebook.com/tia.wrightbottum

Instagram
@timemarkerphotography
@tiascrazylife
@legacylivingwithtia

THANK YOU OFFER

5 Steps to Clearing Money Clutter and Free Assessment and Discovery Call to find out your top three Sacred Money Archetypes via her website, www.timemarkerlegacy.com

Kaylee McDonald

I CAN SEE CLEARLY…NOW

You never know when your life is going to change in an instant, for better or worse…what matters is how you handle it and where you go from there!

There I was, August 2, 2008, on River Canyon Run at Great Wolf Lodge celebrating my oldest daughter's 10th birthday, and I felt this weird thing. To this day I cannot explain what I felt, but I must have looked off enough that my husband instantly asked me if I was ok. I thought I just had some chlorine in my eyes, and it would be fine when I got my contacts out. Boy, did I misdiagnose myself with that one! By the next morning, I was pretty much blind in my left eye. Since I was a physician, I thought I could manage things myself but went into a local Lenscrafters type place (it was a Saturday so my long-time optometrist was not in the office) and was almost immediately sent out with instructions to go straight to the closest ER. Those are never words anyone wants to hear, especially a naturopathic physician who has lived a pretty healthy life.

Ultimately, I diagnosed myself before the MRI, which showed lesions in my brain and the diagnosis of Multiple Sclerosis. I admit I spent the first few weeks in bed; crying and feeling sorry for myself. I closed the office for a week or so since it took me a long time to get used to seeing with only one eye working correctly. At the time, my beautiful daughters were 10 and 6 and all I could think was: "will I be able to SEE them walk down the aisle?"

Two weeks after my diagnosis I needed to fly to Arizona for the American Association of Naturopathic Physicians (AANP) annual conference and I figured being around so many amazing Naturopaths would be the best healing place during this time, so I still went. It was there that my world changed even more dramatically. I reconnected with several colleagues and fellow physicians and reviewed my situation. First, I was told to stop gluten immediately! What?! I am an east coast Jewish girl who loves her bagels, pizza slices and Dunkin Donuts, how on earth can I give up gluten? When I looked at the reality of what could happen if I continued to eat gluten, it was an easy choice. Although, I have tested that decision a few times and usually ended up with a yucky attack, so gluten free I remain after 11 years. Trust me, I still miss my bagels and Dunkin Donuts, but they aren't worth the MS flare that comes right after eating them and historically ends me in the hospital or bed for days or weeks.

Then, I was talking with a fellow physician and she uttered words that changed me forever. She asked what was wrong and I said that I had MS. Pretty basic words, right? Her response was, "Wow! I cannot believe that you are just accepting that as truth." My reply of MRI results, lesions and partially blind was clarified further by her, "so at the moment you are MSing, but do you really want to own the diagnosis?"

I hope, that somewhere deep within me, I would have come to that idea on my own but it was just what I needed to hear at the time. The decision to go to that convention was a great decision. I left Arizona, still MSing, still partially blind, still gluten free, but no longer living by the diagnosis of MS.

ANYTHING IS POSSIBLE

Trust me when I say that having a diagnosis of a chronic disease is not easy, especially one that the symptoms are not obvious. Actually, chronic diseases are a struggle because most of the time you can put on your big girl panties and get through the day without anyone knowing you have any struggles. When something happens, it is often a shock to those around you that you suffer from any diagnosis because you "look so healthy".

To go around everyday wondering "what if" or "when" will lead you living your life in fear and not for the moment. Within a few months of my diagnosis I decided I was going to write a book about MS entitled, "I Can See Clearly Now", but I had not reached out to CCR for title permission and it never got much further than a few chapters. I thought I would pull one of those chapters for this book, but I have grown so much personally since then and it seemed like wasted words. The one area that I loved is that I had "Disney mommy advice" in each chapter for other mothers struggling with a newfound diagnosis. Disney because, I love Disney, and doesn't Disney make everything better? They were suggestions I had to help moms (and dads) not let the diagnosis interfere with the carefree joyful lives their children deserve. Sadly, they were things I learned the hard way. The first few years were not the prettiest in our home and I struggled to get through some days. I still have huge "mommy guilt" over not getting past things sooner and seeing my girls struggle with my battles.

You all know the saying, "Put on a Happy Face", right? Well, when a side of your body does not work or you cannot even dress yourself, that becomes difficult to do. After looking at my daughters growing up in the shadow of a yucky disease, I knew that even though it was super hard, I could not let my down days show on my face or attitude. I needed to show these young women that anything is possible if you decide it is true.

One time, about 2 years after my initial diagnosis, I was "MSing" again and this time had bell's palsy. You are correct if you think this isn't necessarily a MS event, but for me it was related to the virus situation in my body, and I needed to treat myself. I did take some time off work, got acupuncture several times a week, treated myself with daily injections (vitamins) and did a few IVs on myself of a nutrient difficult to take orally for optimal absorption. Yes, I can give myself my own IVs (thankfully). Scott needs to help me with the IVs and at one point I just started laughing. In our bathroom we had needles, syringes and the likes and I could just imagine the girls going into school talking about how they say mommy shooting stuff in her arm (IV push) or her leg (B vitamin injection)! That would have been an interesting thing to recover from in our small community…the local physician seen doing "drugs" at home with her children around! What that moment taught me is that the truth is priceless. Rather than trying to hide things from my daughters, I needed to be open and honest with them and tell them the truth. Scott and I had struggled deciding how much information to tell the girls or allow them to be involved in, but after that realization, I stopped. I let them see my struggles but also my wins. I let them see me in pain but also my ability to move past it all. I let them see my good days and my bad days. I also let them know they were loved and would always be loved no matter what was happening with my health.

I even decided to let them go to a local camp for children whose parents have MS. That was hard for me because it meant they would really learn all the ups and downs of my diagnosis. Well, the first thing they told me when they got in the car, after they talked about how much fun they had, was "Mommy, guess what? It isn't your fault you are a bitch!" Forgive the language but those were the words from my adorable daughters. They were taught that often the lesions will do things to the brain and it makes me snappier, so we took that and turned it into our joke. Scott, Jaide or Taylor would simply have to say turtle and I would know that I was being snappy and needed to take a moment to myself. Showing the full story is difficult but worth it, hiding is never the answer.

In the first few years of my diagnosis, everything was a learning process. The biggest thing I learned was that I needed to listen to my body (but don't we all need to do that?). I would have these minimal and unusual symptoms which usually happen when I was super tired or stressed and I began to take them as signs to slow down or get out for a run (my way of managing stress and helping to control this disease).

RUN FORWARD

Run, did I really say run? Why would someone with a condition that dramatically affects their ability to walk start running? I was a runner in undergrad and through medical school, but somewhere along the ride, my knees started bothering me so it was suggested I find alternative exercise options due to my runners knee. Well, 2 years after my diagnosis, at the end of another facial palsy, I think this one was cranial nerve 6 palsy, a girlfriend asked me if I wanted to run the Princess Half Marathon at Disney World. Ummm, a chance to go to Disney with Scott and without kids, Yes Please! Now, running is not something you just start doing from nothing. It takes dedication, training and willpower. I downloaded an app on my phone (I think it was called MiCoach) and just started running 3-4 times a week. I noticed that I had more energy and was feeling good most days. Could it be that exercise had that much of impact on my disease? As I have already talked about 3 or 4 flares in my first 2 years of diagnosis, since then, I have had approximately 2 more major flares where my left side stopped working in the following 10 years. What has been consistent in those 10 years? Running. The next key thing I learned in this journey is that you need to take care of yourself by managing stress levels. Exercise is one the best solution for stress management, self-care is key and I believe that is why my disease has been so minimal in the past 10 years (knock on wood).

So, my friend asked me to join her running the Disney Princess Half Marathon and of course I said yes. I trained for 7 months, completed a sub hour 10K in December and figured I was ready. I lucked out and was chosen to participate in the run Disney Meet Up (great memories and I really miss those Meet Ups) with Jeff Galloway. That meet-up further changed my life. What I didn't mention is that the whole time I trained, I was running by myself and swore that this would be a one and done thing (well kind of since I had already signed up for the Disneyland Half Marathon 6 months later) but that was it. Then, I got to Disney and met all these amazing people at the meet up and found a new tribe. A group of people who were supportive and so full of love. At this point, 11 years after I completed my first half marathon (2/26/12 with a time of 2:07) I have completed approximately 43 half marathons, 1 full marathon and multiple 10K and 5K races. Training is still difficult, but crossing that finish line is the best feeling, especially knowing that MS has not dictated my life ever! Every run I finish, I smile and look up and let my uncle Joel, the father figure in my life who we lost way too young to MS, know that I was doing this for me but in his memory.

If I can offer anything to my patients, those reading this chapter and even my friends and family, it is to take every moment, find the positive and run forward – never backwards. When I first got diagnosed, I was terrified about what would happen if my community or my patients found out that I was diagnosed with MS. What would they think? Would they assume I am unable to practice? OK, that is the silliest thing ever. Worrying about what other people think about you, what a waste of time! Remember, people do not have the time to think or worry about you, they care about themselves. This is not meaning to sound rude, but as the comparison trap has exploded over the recent years with the growth of social media, it has made me realize I need to live my life for me (and my family) but not really care or worry about what others think. I still struggle with the idea of not "caring" what others think about me, but I realize that the thought of what they think about me is all in my head and they probably do not even think about me at all.

As I got more involved with the MS community in 2012 and 2013, I realized that showing up in high heels (my shoes of choice in warm weather and the higher the better) with a smile on my face and taking on life with no constraints was the best thing I could do for fellow MS patients. To this day, almost 12.5 years later, I still have long time patients come in and say how shocked they are to learn I have MS. I do not hide this anymore, but I also don't advertise it. Many patients let me know that watching how I handle this disease has helped them get through tough days.

Getting a life changing diagnosis, or any bad news really, you have a few directions you can go, and your future depends on the next steps you take. I challenge you to stop, take a deep breathe and really think about what is in front of you and how you can handle it. Don't let it derail your future, let it be the stepping stone to your successful and healthy future!

I must have done something right because both of my daughters (now 22 and 19) wrote college essays about me - my strength and determination and how it helped shape them into the wonderful young women they have become. Hopefully, they were not just words to get them into their schools and they really meant it!

Each day is a journey, and every moment is a step forward. Let me end with some great Disney quotes that have gotten me through those dark days…

"Believe you can, then you will" Mulan

"If you focus on what you left behind, you will never be able to see what lies ahead" Gusteau

"All our dreams can come true, if we have the courage to pursue them" W Disney

"The way to get started is to quit talking and begin doing" W Disney

And my all time favorite…

"It's kind of fun to do the impossible" W Disney

Find your own quotes to live by and do not let anyone tell you that you cannot – for you can do anything if you believe in yourself and the power of your body. So, go soar and succeed and thrive!

Much Love…Kaylee

ACKNOWLEDGEMENTS

This chapter is a labor of love that began in 2011 and thanks to The Fabulous Dorris was brought out of me in 2020. Thank you to all those who have supported me on this crazy MS journey, especially Joyce, Jaide, Taylor and my love, Scott. Their love and support, along with my circle of friends and family (too many to name individually), make it easy to keep plugging along. I also want to give a shout our to Mema and Uncle Joel who showed me how to fight from the beginning and I can feel with me, especially on the hard days.

ABOUT AUTHOR

Dr Kaylee McDonald is a Naturopathic Physician in Washington State who had her life take a turn when she lost her vision in one eye and refocused on the healing power of nature and Doctor Heal Thyself. She has been in private practice since 1997 and has enjoyed 25 years as a physician helping guide others on their path to wellness.

ABOUT MY BUSINESS

Dr. McDonald started her college career with the goal of being a pediatrician. Although she has never strayed from her desire to be a physician, her practice over the years has taken many turns so that she can be the best physician for her patients. Currently, she focuses on aging optimally with a focus on hormone optimization and helping people realize getting old doesn't mean feeling lousy.

Website
www.RainerNaturalHealthClinic.com

Facebook Personal Page
Facebook.com/kaylee.n.mcdonald.7

Twitter
Drkaylee

Instagram
@Drkaylee

THANK YOU

Local to WA state readers: 50.00 off initial pellets (after labs and consultation appointment) To all readers: sign up for email list and get initial list of top 10 tips for living your best life - health and wellness tips.

Susan Lataille

HONOR – HOPE – HAPPINESS

My life changed forever on March 9, 2017, at 4:04 am, with the last breath of my son. A piece of me; gone forever. That piece will always and forever remain with Nathan. What now? I had to figure out how to continue to live my life without my son being here. I believe that our relationship and connection will continue only in a much different way. I still need and want to feel that connection. That will never end.

As in everything in my life I started my grief process was gratitude. Not for what happened, but how it happened. The three top gratitude's were first, that he came home to me to care for him instead of staying in Michigan with his dad's family, second that his last words were "I love you, Mom" which I will always treasure, and lastly for the honor of being the only one in his hospital room when he passed, only minutes before his dad and stepmother came into the room. There are so many memories that I hold dear, the wonderful, happy ones as well as the difficult ones.

Our story begins on June 23, 1988, at 10:55 pm, the time of my son's birth in Rota, Spain. While I was in the US Navy, I was married, got pregnant very shortly afterward, and discharged; while my husband at the time finished his tour of duty. Nathan was born on the Naval Base, which started our very special journey of almost 29 years together.

I never thought I could love anyone this much! This boy was such a gift; he was so very special to me. My life changed forever in an instant. I was amazed at the age of 22 that I actually gave birth to this incredible child. I spent the first 6 months with him at almost every moment of our lives. I felt a special connection to him that will last forever.

His life started off with struggling with colic, being an infant and new mother was a challenge for both of us. Plus, we were in Spain with no family for assistance. At moments, I wasn't sure what to do or how to help him. As he grew out of the colic phase, he became a truly happy child. He was always smiling, once he started walking there was no stopping him. All he wanted to do was go until he finally collapsed into sleep wherever he was at the moment. Sleeping always came easy to him and remained that way throughout his life. He could literally sleep anywhere including the floor! Most nights, I was carrying him off to bed.

At the early age of 2 ½, his father and I decided on a mutually agreeable split and divorced a year later. This was so difficult for him as he wanted to be with both of us. I remember each time upon returning from a visit with his father I would hold him in my arms as he would cry. I felt everything he did, so I cried along with him. This was the first time I wished that I could take his pain away. My heart broke for him every time and continues to when I think of his suffering.

His Dad was a career Navy man and spent many years living in Virginia Beach. He would visit his dad and family on holiday weeks and vacations. He started flying at the age of 5. I'll never forget the first time he flew. The flight attendant took his hand, he said goodbye, and went without turning back. Every time he left, I cried. I'd stand in the terminal until his plane left the gate and took off. I would talk to him as often as possible while he was away. This pattern continued until the age of 13 when due to many circumstances with school and classmates, we all decided, my son, his dad, and I, that he would live with his dad and go to school in Michigan. His father had since retired Navy and went back to his home state. That was an extremely difficult decision to make. I wanted to do what was best for him not for me. As it would turn out, I was able to spend more quality time when he did visit me on holidays and vacations. We remained in contact talking at least once a week. I missed him so much while he was gone. It was like a piece of me was missing. I think he was starting to prepare me for living without him.

There's always been such an incredible bond between us. I was so proud when he graduated from high school. It was a tough road for him to be diagnosed with ADHD at the age of six. Sports helped him get through school. He always loved sports, playing, and watching. It gave him something to focus on and a way to burn off energy.

While I questioned being a good mother many times, I do know that I love him more than life itself. If I could be with him now, I would go without hesitation.

THERE WAS SOMETHING GOING ON

After graduation, he struggled with keeping jobs. Since school wasn't for him, he decided not to go to college. It just wasn't in the picture. I also believe at this time he started to struggle due to the tumor starting to grow in his brain. He would bounce back and forth between Rhode Island and Michigan. He worked at a country club while living with me and then in the offseason going back to stay with his dad. It was always so hard for him to choose where he wanted to be. He had family and friends in both locations. Everywhere he went everyone loved him. He had a huge heart and was always aware of everyone's feelings and would have given the shirt off his back. He put others before himself even in the end.

There was about a two-year period that I didn't see him. He was having a really difficult time finding a job in Michigan so he and his girlfriend at the time decided to go to Key West, Florida where her parents lived. He managed to find a job at a local hotel, barely making ends meet. His girlfriend broke up with him that made things worse. Occasionally, he would call and ask for money so that he could eat. My heart was breaking. Again, I wanted to take away his pain. Finally, on persistence from his father, he returned to Michigan after a year.

Leading up to his diagnosis, in April 2014 he came back home to me because his dad and stepmother didn't know how to cope with him anymore. He was extremely confrontational and unreasonable. Upon returning home, I could clearly see that there was something going on with him. I knew was he wasn't the affectionate, loving, and respectful son I knew. He continued to struggle with finding and keeping a job. He had no drive to do anything and was sleeping a lot.

I knew he was in pain. I thought that maybe it was because of his teeth. He did go to urgent care once and they gave him pain medication that only made his aggression skyrocket. After him taking them for a few days I managed to get to the bottle and put it down the garbage disposal. He was furious! And I was at my end. I just didn't know what to do or think at this point. I knew he needed help and I didn't know how to help him. He refused to go to the doctor. One of his friends actually brought him to the Emergency Room one night and he refused treatment.

On November 7, 2014, my husband and I were getting ready to leave for vacation for a week on Cape Cod. I had continued to strongly suggest that he go to the doctor. He was afraid to know the outcome. Before I left that day, I said to him, "I don't know what's going on with you, but if you won't do it for yourself please do it for me." That night, he had a seizure while driving on a side street and hit a few cars. Gratefully, he wasn't hurt in the accident. When the police arrived, they transported him to the hospital not knowing what was wrong with him, as he wasn't drunk. He didn't remember much of what happened when I questioned him weeks later.

At 2 am, I received a phone call from Johnston police, saying that my son was in an accident and I needed to call the nurse at Woonsocket Hospital. When I spoke to the nurse, she told me that they found a large mass on his brain and they would be transporting him to Rhode Island

Hospital as soon as possible. I was in complete disbelief and wasn't even sure what I was supposed to do. I was in shock! I told my husband and then called my brother (who stays up late and I've always been very close to) to tell him what had happened. I then laid down attempting to absorb what I was just told. After only a moment, I jumped up saying, we need to go. We packed up, loaded the car, and made it home in record time.

On the ride home, I was not sure what to think. My thoughts raced to so many possibilities and outcomes including that my son wouldn't see his 27th birthday. How could this be happening? I remember thinking before this happened that I was grateful for not having to experience any tragedy in my life up to now. Boy did this makeup for it!

When we arrived at the hospital, he was so sedated and having seizures after seizures. I couldn't believe his condition. I did my best to comfort him by talking softly and touch his arm or leg. I so wanted to take away his pain. I wanted this nightmare to be over! I wanted to hold him and make everything better. My inside were torn apart, while I kept a strong outside presence.

They kept running different tests and finally onto an MRI. I was grateful, they let my husband and I go into the waiting area. Once the MRI was complete, we were told to go to the 6th floor waiting area and they would get him settled into a room. Again, I was standing in the waiting area not sure what to think or feel. I was ready to scream!

My husband decided to go home at that point to shower and eat. I was alone and scared to know what was next. Being alone made my thoughts go in all different directions again. The surgeon came to see me and explained that Nathan needed to go in for emergency surgery and he was pulling a team together. It was about 5 am on Saturday morning so his staff was off for the weekend. He also told me that he would treat him as if he was his own son and gave me a hug. I was touched by the compassion of his surgeon. I'll never forget his kindness at one of the worst moments of my life.

I was so grateful for how everything happened knowing that so many different scenarios could have changed everything. If the tumor continued to grow it would have killed him instantly.

Next, I had to call his father in Michigan. I didn't even have his phone number. Strangely enough, it turned out my brother had it from many years ago. That was such an odd call. Very awkward, I didn't even recognize his voice. It had been so long since I've spoken to him. When I asked for Ed, he wanted to know who was calling. I replied Nate's mother. Then I proceeded to give him as many of the details as I recalled. I was in disbelief that all of this was happening and the words that were coming out of my mouth! All I could think is that I needed to be strong for everyone else. I tend to put everyone else before attending to my own needs.

He went into surgery, and I went home to shower before returning to the hospital waiting area for the surgeon to come and tell us how it went. The minutes felt like days. Finally, the wait was over, his surgery was successful, although the entire tumor couldn't be removed due to the location. We could go up to the 6th floor waiting area until he was settled into a room.

I was so grateful that he was strong. It was still so hard to believe that he just went through brain surgery. He was still sedated when we were able to go to his room. It took most of the day for him to become conscious somewhat because he was given so much pain medication.

He pulled through that surgery with flying colors. It was amazing how quickly he recovered and was released from the hospital within 3 days. He was only 26 years old at this time and still so full of life. His dad and stepmother arrived early the next day after driving all night. It was strange seeing this man and his wife. My son called her Mom, as he had known her since he was 3 years old. I gave them the space to spend the time with him as he was recovering in Neurology ICU. He was able to come home after a few days to continue his recovery.

HONORING HIS WISHES

The next 2 ½ years were up and down as he went through treatment and recovery. Visiting his dad as he was able and returning for doctor's appointments and other services to me. It was so hard to witness him going through chemotherapy and radiation. My sweet boy was hardly recognizable due to the effects of the tumor and surgery except when he texted me. We texted every single day that he wasn't with me in the morning and at night. I still keep a copy of the text messages. In his message, I could feel a glimpse of that sweet boy I've always known. Occasionally, I revisit those messages. I miss him so much!

God definitely has a sense of humor, as I'm very

holistic in nature to have to watch my son go through the mainstream medical craziness. I believe in my heart that he came home to me because I allowed him to go through his process, as he needed to without interfering. I had to honor his wishes even when they conflicted with my own beliefs. I incorporated holistic modalities when it was possible to support his journey.

I wanted him to start thinking about the future. He mentioned going to school a few times but I think it was just to appease us. I believe that he knew he wouldn't be around much longer and was spending as much time as possible with those he loved.

He was good at telling everyone what he or she wanted to hear except for me. He knew that I was the one person that he didn't have to pretend. I remember questioning why he was so different in front of some people. I realized that he was showing them what they wanted to see while hiding what was really going on.

A full-blown seizure on July 4, 2016 while in Michigan was the first sign that his tumor had started growing again. His father experienced was it was like being with him in the hospital. He could be a handful. When I saw his stepmother calling me, I went into an instant panic. I was a mess waiting for a report from the emergency room. He was so far away from me. Surprisingly, the CAT Scan didn't show anything so he remained in Michigan for two more months.

Upon having an MRI when he returned home in September, the results showed that it had grown to a sizeable tumor once again. Going through all the motions preparing for surgery was grueling. He had many doctors' appointments, tests, pre-operation, etc. His second surgery was just about 2 years to the day on November 15, 2016. This surgery was so much different as we were all prepared. The surgery went great although again the surgeon wasn't able to remove the entire tumor. It also affected his speech in a way that the words just didn't come out the way he was thinking them. This was very frustrating for him that he stopped talking unless he really needed to.

Upon receiving the pathology, we learned that he now had Stage 4 Cancer called Glioblastoma. We looked at all options including radiation and chemotherapy so he could decide on the best course of action for him. I presented him with all the options and let him decide. I continued to want this to be his journey. He started treatment shortly afterward. Everything seemed to move so slowly.

Within 6 weeks, I could see that he was starting to decline and asked for an MRI. An MRI couldn't be scheduled without first seeing his oncologist. It took several weeks to get an appointment, then several more weeks to get an MRI, and a few more days to get the results. I was frustrated that so much time was going by between appointments. Nathan was declining quickly.

Finally, at a last resort, I found a company in California that sold cannabis. They had great results with different types of cancer including the same diagnoses as my son. I had hoped it would help him as well. As it turned out nothing I did helped him. He steadily declined despite all the different modalities I tried. Starting at the end of December, each week he declined more. He started to lose weight and forget things. It was so hard to watch as he forgot how to use the remote control and completely stopped using his phone. He used to always be listening to music or texting friends. I stayed patient and explained how to use things.

About two weeks before he passed I was finally able to get some services in the home. I wish his doctors had given me this information sooner. I had to call and request the additional services.

By the end of February, I was completely exhausted. I had been working from home in the morning before I got him up. I would let him sleep until about 11 am before having him come upstairs to eat. By this point, I would have to help him up the stairs, as he wasn't able to do it on his own. Most of the time, I didn't even think about what was happening, as I was only focused on what needed to be done. About this time my husband asked me "How long was I going to do this?" my reply was "As long as I need to". It didn't matter at this point. All I could think of was caring for him.

I wanted to support him in all ways so I created a GoFundMe account to help with the cost of holistic modalities that his health insurance wouldn't cover. The response was incredible. I appreciated every donation that was given. This allowed me to let go of some of the money worries. Also, at this time one of his uncles was planning a fundraiser to help him. I was so very touched that so many wanted to help.

Three days before his passing I wanted to have my friend Colleen visit to do some drumming with him. I had asked him several months before and he was so against it.

I was hoping that it could help him in some way. That morning, I let him know what was happening. I thought he would just want to stay downstairs. As it turns out, I went to check on him before Colleen arrived and he was standing in his room. I hadn't seen him stand on his own in weeks. I said, "ok, let's get you dressed and upstairs for some breakfast". I reminded him again that Colleen was coming and if he wanted to go back downstairs he would have to let me know. Colleen arrived, I introduced him to her, and he finished his breakfast. He sat there and absorbed the energy and vibration of the drumming. I tried to relax but all I could think of was how he was doing. I kept opening my eyes to watch him. Colleen left shortly afterward saying that she would call me.

A few hours later Colleen did call. She told me that he was 60% over on the other side although still undecided. Also, she said that his aura was what appeared to be liquid. It was something she had never seen before now. I wasn't sure what to think of all of this.

That night, as I was putting him to bed I told him that I loved him. His response, usually the only thing he said, was "I love you, Mom". He just stared at me. I left him disappointed and came back a while later before going to bed. I needed to change him and again, I told him I loved him. I was so happy that he responded. It was the last time he spoke to say "I love you Mom". I'll forever be grateful that those were his last words.

The next morning, I wasn't able to get him to open his eyes. I had a really hard time getting him up the stairs because he wasn't able to help. The CNA bathed him and got him dressed all while he had his eyes shut. We sat him in the chair, he seemed to know I was there but wasn't able to respond. Shortly after the CNA left, I received a call from his nurse. She told me that his non-responsiveness was indicating something was seriously wrong and to call 9-1-1. I went into an instant panic and then did as I was told. I immediately called my husband to let him know what was happening and texted his father and stepmother. I was shaking as they loaded him into the back of the rescue and I was instructed to get in front. Was this really happening?

We arrived at the hospital, answered a series of questions, and then waited. They started to check him and then he headed off to have an MRI. As it turned out his tumor had grown to the point where it was putting so much pressure on his brain that it was affecting everything. They gave him medication to help relieve the pressure. At about 8 pm was the last time he opened his eyes for a short time.

The next day was so tough. He was having seizure after seizure. Nothing the hospital staff was doing seemed to be helping. I kept asking the nurses if they could do anything for him. Finally, later in the day, I asked my husband to bring me his cannabis. I started to give him small doses. That seems to help him settle.

Earlier in the day, I had asked my friend Colleen to come and give him his last rights, as I knew that it wouldn't be much longer. The timing couldn't have been more perfect as she arrived moments after Nate's father and stepmother left for the night. It was simple and appropriate for him. She always seems to come up with the perfect words.

Finally, at about 11 pm, I decided to go home and get some sleep asking the nurse on duty to call me if anything changed. He seemed to be comfortable and stable.

I went home and finally fell asleep when at about 3 am the phone rang. It was the hospital telling me that I needed to come back as his breathing was labored. I called his dad and headed back to the hospital. Upon arrival, the nurse asked me if they had permission to make him comfortable, which meant morphine. I then sat on his bed with my hand on his heart. I spoke to him softly, telling him how much I loved him knowing that the time was near. After about 20 minutes, he took one last breath. It was so loud it scared me.

I sit there for a few more minutes wondering if he's actually gone. His father and stepmother walk into the room a few minutes later disturbing my special time. I left the room going to give them some private time with him. As I walked up to the nurse's station, the nurse on duty asks me if I know he's gone. My reply is that I wasn't sure. I asked her about the time of death. The reply was 4:04 am. That sounded like a special number to me. I then have to walk back into the room to tell his father and stepmother that he's gone. I'm in disbelief. I deliver the message, his father breaks down and his stepmother says "but he's still warm". I waited around a few more minutes and then left them to have some time alone with him. In hindsight, I wish I had stayed a bit longer. I was thinking that he's gone so there's no need to stay. The nurse asked if I was okay to drive home. My reply was yes. I was relieved for him that he no longer had to suffer and heartbroken at the same time. "Is this real? How is this possible"?

I NEEDED TO BE STRONG

As I left the hospital, in disbelief, how could this be happening? How could he be gone? I arrive home and my husband looked at me knowing that he'd passed before I told him. He held me although I wasn't able to break down. I thought I needed to be strong for everyone. A part of me was relieved that I didn't have to watch him suffer any longer. He had been through so much over the past 5-6 years. The other part of me would have taken care of him forever.

I tried to get some sleep. That wasn't happening. A little bit after 7 am the phone rang. It was New England Donor wanting to ask me questions about my son because unknown to me he was an organ donor. It seemed so surreal talking about him as I answered a series of questions that went on for about 20 minutes. I was proud of my son that he had offered his organs to help others. Even in death, he was thinking of others. His corneas were taken which gave two other people sight and a better quality of life. It warms my heart to know that a part of him lives on. His eyes were beautiful. Even in his last day of life, the nurse commented on his eyes.

I was amazed at how I could no longer feel his energy. His room felt cold and it hurt so much not being able to feel him. This was so unexpected for me. The realization that he was gone, hit me so hard.

Somehow, I went through the motions of the day, asking my husband to call the funeral home, going to the appointment, and make his final arrangements along with his father. I was grateful that he gave me the freedom to do what I thought was best. I wanted to do a celebration of life after he was cremated. Thank God for the fundraisers that helped pay for his final expenses. I didn't have to worry about the money along with the grief.

The following Saturday, I invited my family over for lunch. Part of my process was to start cleaning out his things. I held onto the things that were special to me, clothing and other items. I gave my family things that I thought they would want. I gave clothes to my nephew along with coffee syrup and wipes along with other items to one of my sisters with small children. I was thinking if I was able to remove some of his belongings that it would somehow remove some of the pain.

I wasn't sure what to do or say. I wasn't sure how to act. I wasn't sure if I could continue without him. I know a piece of my heart died with him that day. I know that we'll always be connected, although that doesn't change the fact that I can't hold him or see him.

I did my best to stay in gratitude. I'm grateful that I was able to care for him. I'm grateful that his last words were "I love you, Mom". I'm grateful that I worked from home. I'm grateful that he came home to me when he needed me most. I'm grateful to have had him for 28 years.

His celebration was held the following weekend. I was grateful to all those who came and my friend Colleen for being the minister. As I welcomed his loved ones to speak, his father went first, followed by my brother, sister, my son's aunt, and then while I didn't think I was going to say anything, I felt like how couldn't I after hearing everyone else.

I thought I was able to say exactly what I wanted.

Saying that I learned so much more from him than he ever did from me. That we bring our children into this world thinking that we're going to teach them everything and in the end, it's us that learns so much. His father used my exact words at his Celebration in Michigan the following month.

I went through the motions of the day. Being strong and holding up well. I was still thinking that I needed to be strong. I didn't know how to allow myself to be comforted by anyone. I didn't cry through the service. I was strong! I could handle it! Boy, was I wrong!

The following month, we drove out to Michigan to attend Nathan's Celebration of Life. He had lived in both places and had touched so many people's lives. Up to attending the Celebration, I thought that I was doing okay until I spent time in the energy of sadness. It put me right back. We didn't stay too long at the service. It was nice to see pictures that I've never seen before from his life there. It was touching and heartfelt. One of my ex-sister-in-laws welcomed me to the group of women who lost children. I didn't want to be part of that group. I wanted to process this on my own. I didn't want to admit that I needed anyone else to help me.

My wellness expo was less than one month from Nate's passing. How was I going to manage getting through that day from set up to close? I did my best to stay busy and only talk to attendees and exhibitors for a very short time. I moved quickly from person to person. I wasn't able to enjoy myself. The event had once been my favorite. I had enjoyed every minute in past events.

Life went on, I continued to work in my business. I

continued to network although I couldn't stay around people very long. I would go and leave within about 30 minutes. Finally, as July approached, I just needed to get away. I needed to be by myself to process. I decided to go to Cape Cod for a few days. My husband didn't understand really but said okay. I dropped my dog off at my mothers' place since my husband worked long days and started on my 90-minute drive. As soon as I pulled away from the curb the tears started flowing, the questions, the anger, and every other emotion that I hadn't allowed myself to feel came flooding out! I was able to release so much emotion. I could hear my son in my head responding to me. Telling me that everything was going to be okay and that it all happened exactly as it was intended. He was grateful for caring for him and everything that I did. He wished that he could still be with me. My heart was broken. A piece of me had died. I didn't feel whole. I didn't know what was going to keep me moving forward.

By the time I arrived on the Cape, the tears had dried and I was feeling a bit better. I unpacked my things into a tiny cottage and wondered what to do next. While I spend my time there I'd read, journal, walked in nature, went to the local coffee shop, and meditated. I did my best to take care of my needs as I was disconnected from everyone. It was a healing time. I found myself not knowing what to do with myself and a bit bored. I felt like I got so much out during the drive. I ended up leaving a day early.

At this point, it's been hard to talk to most people about my experience even my husband. I believe that he doesn't completely understand not having children of his own. It's been hard to continue to live. Life looks so different. Little things are no longer important. I only want to have conversations that are meaningful and not superficial. Networking is hard with most business professionals. Small talk loses my interest.

Life goes on. I just go through the motions. Right before Christmas, I kept asking Nate was he was giving me. Two days before I received a check for a little over $600 from the State of Rhode Island for back child support. This was from seventeen years ago. I was shocked and amazed! All I could say was "Thank you, Nate"!

My sisters' wedding was the following year. I was a bride's maid. Grief came down like a crashing wave. I don't think it crossed my mind until we were all standing during the vows and seeing my new brother-in-law's grandson there all dressed up in a suit did it remind me of Nate. I barely held it together. I was thinking that Nate should have been there. It was hard to be part of a celebration when I felt broken. My sister had a picture of her and Nathan. It's one of my favorites. Luckily after the ceremony, we all went outside to leave for pictures in another location so that I could compose myself. I did share with my husband. He knew, he always knows without me saying anything.

My husband and I sold our townhouse in June 2018. The day of our closing I was a total mess. As I said goodbye, to each room all the memories of my son being there came flowing back. My husband and I drove separately to the closing attorney's office. As I drove, I told myself to keep it together until after the closing and I was on my way to Cape Cod. It was so hard. A few tears fell on my cheeks. I wouldn't allow myself to breakdown. I also didn't share what I was going through with my husband. I just didn't know how to and part of me just wanted to keep it to myself.

So many times have I kept it all in not thinking that anyone wants to hear anything about how I'm feeling. It was hard keeping it all-in-all the time. I've been such a private person for so long probably because when I was in my 20s I talked about the same thing over and over and thought I lost friends because of it.

Living on Cape Cod for the summer had its blessings as well as a lot of time to think since I was there and my husband was in Rhode Island except on the weekends.

Moving to Foster on August 17, 2018, was different. I wish Nate were here. I kept saying to him that there's so much he could have done to help especially with the landscaping.

My birthday on September 21, 2018, was a particularly hard day for me. I had scheduled time with some friends for coffee and then for lunch. As I drove to the coffee shop my heart felt heavy. I only shared a bit with my friends. By lunchtime, I was a basket case. I finally shared what I was going through and broke down at a friend of a friend's home that I stopped by to visit. I just couldn't keep it in any longer.

Grief has hit me every significant day including Nate's anniversary of his passing, birthday, my birthday, and holidays as well as special occasions. It's always hard. Grief is always just one moment away. It always feels like my heart is broken. It always feels like I'm not sure if I can go on or why? Somehow, I do find a way because there are so many wonderful things and people in my life.

This story begins with honor. It's about honoring him along his journey. While I would have loved to change it, I knew in my heart that he was meant to go. I had to honor him and his wishes. It's also about honoring myself to go through the grief process in my own way.

Next is hope, for me to able to continue with a purpose. It's been very difficult for me to figure out what truly makes me happy while living a life with purpose. I keep wondering how to take my experiences to help others. The year 2020 was significant, as I started to discover more of who I am and what I wanted. I looked at all that I've learned up to this point in my life including those hard lessons while caring for my son.

I learned first that it's okay to ask for help. In the beginning, I felt that I needed to do it all on my own. I finally realized that I needed help and there were those people more than willing to do so. We're not meant to do it alone. It was very touching for so many friends to come to my aid.

What I learned next was true compassion. This wasn't easy for me to show others compassion. Along the way, I somehow believed that it was our own fault for being in any situation. While I still believe that is true in most circumstances, it's important to show others compassion. Part of me had become very hard and put up a wall from my own life experiences. I think because I feel too much and it overwhelmed me. I've been getting better knowing that I am safe.

One of the hardest things for me is to show people who I really am. There are very few people who I've cried in front of through my grieving process. I felt that I need to be strong. While I know that's not true, I find it hard to break away from it many times.

IT'S ABOUT HAPPINESS

Life has had its ups and downs in this process of discovery. There were many days that I just didn't find that I cared about too many things. I found myself wondering what it was all about while witnessing circumstances that others would get upset by or listening to conversations that seemed insignificant. I thought life just has to have more meaning.

In learning more about myself, I realized that I held onto a business for years that I wanted to exit. At the time, I felt that it was a safe place and a security net. Also, it felt like it was something I could control and do with confidence. I wasn't ready to move on to the unknown yet.

In 2020, that safety net was taken away through the pandemic. I'm very grateful that it helped me move forward. It gave me the ability to start looking for new opportunities. I learned quickly that many weren't what I wanted until I connected with a woman in Colorado. I began to learn so much from her that the entire course of my life has changed. I was ready.

Living alongside grief has made me become more compassionate, deliberate, and forgiving. It's made me look at life in a whole new light. I now look at trivial circumstances and drama as insignificant. I spend little time thinking about things that aren't important. I look for purpose in all that I do. I've thought since the beginning of my grief that I was meant to help others with grief as well. I know that since I'm still here walking this earth that I have a mission.

As I write this story, I feel closer to finding my purpose and feeling needed. One of the things I miss the most is being actively Nate's mother. The sense of truly being needed died with him. I'm still his mother although I don't need to mother him any longer. Helping others brings me joy. Currently, I'm working on a program to help children and their families.

In my search to help others, writing this story is another step. I hope that you, dear reader, find some inspiration and know that you are not alone in your grief. So many times I have felt like I was silently grieving. We truly never know what's going on in someone's life. When someone is experiencing a "bad day", I always think that there's something bigger hidden behind their behavior. I give them grace and know that it has nothing to do with me.

One of the intentions is to start a podcast series called "Conversations with Susan" to host others that have lost a loved one to share their process. These are conversations to help shine a light on grief. Talking about grief and our loved ones is so important. Unfortunately, it's still a taboo subject as many people are not sure how to be open about it. It helps me to talk about how special he is and share stories. It's not always easy to find someone willing to listen. I love to talk about my son and to share tools that I use that have helped me along my path. This brings me joy and the connection I so miss.

My hope is that I will be able to continue to live alongside my grief and help others at the same time. I believe that grief is not linear. It can show itself at any moment. The smallest things remind me of him. It's like a wave crashing down on me. I never know when it's going to hit. In the moment it feels like it just happened and I'm still in disbelief.

My life is about living it to its fullest and being of service to others. I admit at times life can be hard when grief comes crashing down when I least expect it. My son is always the next possible thought. I give myself permission to continue to grieve in my own way.

I've questioned my existence many, many times. Recently I've wanted to start my life with a clean slate. The year of 2020 has all been about discovery for me. It's included the discovery of who I am now; discovery in life and the work that makes me happy; and discovery of how to continue my life with purpose. Every day I learn something new about myself. It's consistent and changes rapidly.

Last, it's about happiness. We all have the right to be happy no matter what has come our way in life. We're here to have experiences and learn from them. It's what we do with those experiences that make us who we have become. Nathan would want me to be happy as any loved one would want for you. He would want me to live a fulfilled life. He would want me to share our story. In the beginning, I was saying my story until I realized that it's our story. It's a love story between a mother and her son.

In the beginning, I had to focus on gratitude. I wasn't sure how to continue or if I wanted to. All I wanted to do was be with him and wonder why him. I knew in my gut that he was going. I would have gladly died in his place. I would have done anything for him. Being a mother was my greatest accomplishment. I am still his mother. We are still connected for eternity. As life continues, I've found pieces of happiness along the way. Currently, I'm very conscious of some things that make me happy. I'm still in search of finding my place in the world. I believe that the journey of discovery will continue throughout my life.

Our story does not end, not here, not ever. Our story is unique to us although I'm sure many have had similar experiences. It's special to me. I hold my memories sacred in my heart and mind. Memories continue as our relationship continues in a different way. I am honored to be his mother.

I honored him. I believe that he came home to me because I allowed him to go through his process, as he needed to when everyone else wanted to fix him.

I knew with every cell in my body that this was meant to be. He came, touched so many lives, everyone loved him, and his smile lit up the room. He would give away everything he had especially money. He always helped others before himself.

Life does truly go on, there's so much beauty in the world when we open our eyes to take a look. I am very fortunate to be surrounded by so many, many amazing, inspiring, and supportive individuals. I wouldn't be where I am now if it weren't for them.

Life can be good when we allow it. It may never be the same again. It can be good in so many different ways. I've always believed that we are meant to do something with our experiences to help others. This is no exception.

I write this in the hope that you, the reader; find a way to live your life to the fullest. Baby steps – one at a time…no matter what your challenges are in life.

I believe that he's still here when I need him most. The signs are real and knowing that I can have conversations with him in my mind when the need arises. This brings me comfort.

There are so many signs and stories to share. The most recent one that really impacted me was a journeying I did at a conference. The journey consisted of getting into a meditative state starting with the time of our death. As I journeyed along I arrived at a holding space where Nate was waiting for me. We had a wonderful time being with each other that I didn't want to leave. I had known if I went further on this journey I would not have come back. It was such an emotional experience. All I wanted to do was cry. It was amazing to feel his presence so strongly. I was grateful for this experience.

There are also many signs. One is that I'm always aware of numbers. I see his birth date when I'm searching for answers. I'm not always sure what they mean although it's comforting. Also, while writing our story, the light on the side table started to flicker even though it wasn't on. I was happy that he made his presence known. Was it a confirmation that he approved of me writing our story?

Thank you Nate for being here as I write this story, our story. We get to choose what we focus on and how we experience life. We create our story. Our story and our love will last for eternity. I look forward to the time we are fully reconnected.

Now go live your life! Find what makes you happy and don't stop until you do.

ACKNOWLEDGMENTS

I would like to acknowledge all of the support I've received from so many friends and family from the time of diagnoses to the current day. There's too many to list and I wouldn't want to leave anyone out. It still amazes me the generosity of those that came to my aid. I am truly grateful.

ABOUT AUTHOR

Susan Lataille is a mother, wife, daughter, sister, entrepreneur, and much more. She became a business owner in 2010 with an event production company producing trade shows and other events. This business came from her passion of the holistic world and that she's a natural connector! Over the course of years she also became a Reiki Master, Full Wave Breath Facilitator, Akashic Records Consultant, Certified International Health Coach, and more. All of these tools helped and continue to help her in the grieving process of her son. In 2020, due to the pandemic, it was time for a change. Time to move onto another business that made her happy and excited. She found something that could tie her passion for the holistic world and her love of animals in a company called PetClub 247.

ABOUT MY BUSINESS

Susan Lataille is currently working on a passion project that combines her passion for anything holistic with her love of all animals with PetClub 247. With the use of natural ingredients that make better treats, foods, and toys for our pets, we are on a mission to help keep our furry best friends around longer! PetClub 247 was born out of a desire to give our pets the long, healthy, happy lives they deserve and to make a healthy diet accessible and affordable to every pet parent. We have created a place we can shop with confidence. We have developed a full line of all-natural (made in the U.S.A.) products that you can only find at PetClub 247, to help keep your fur kid by your side for longer. All the natural support your pet needs, in one place.

Website
http://happy.petclub247.com

Facebook Personal Page
https://www.facebook.com/susan.lataille/

ACKNOWLEDGMENTS

It takes a village to produce a book, and I am deeply grateful for the creative forces and dedication of every single person who added her or his magic to this one.

This is the sixth book in our Don't Be Invisible Be Fabulous series – and I am deeply honored.

My whole-hearted appreciation starts with the readers and supporters of our first, best-selling book; they inspired the second, third, fourth, fifth and now sixth volume. This journey reinforced in my bones how essential it is to tell stories of real-life women triumphing in their lives. Thousands of women saw themselves in those stories, and then they could imagine a way forward in their own lives. So, of course, Volume 6, featuring more stories of hope and inspiration, had to be born!

Heaps of appreciation also go to the fabulous coauthors from our first, second, third, fourth and fifth books:

Thank you all!

WELCOME TO FAB FACTOR
Don't Be Invisible, Be Fabulous!
LEARN MORE

The Entrance To The World Of Elevating Your Self-Image

An Invitation From The Fabulous Dorris Burch.

I would be honored to have you in our ever-expanding circle! Here are a few ways to be involved.

RESOURCES

Programs

HOW 12 WEEKS OF LIVE YOUR LIFE IN STYLE WILL CHANGE YOUR LIFE
IMAGINE THIS…
You open your closet, and you know exactly what you want to wear. Better yet, you're excited to get dressed. You

walk into work (whether that's on the job at home or in the office) feeling like a total BOSS. You know no matter where you are and what you're doing, your outfit is showing the best version of you.

BY THE END OF OUR JOURNEY TOGETHER, YOU'LL HAVE:
- Learned what works in your closet and what doesn't.
- Tried (and loved) new things outside of your style zone.
- Learned your own tricks to find energy to get dressed in a snap.
- Gained the confidence to wear what you want and feel good wearing it.
- Documented what you like and why, so you can start building your closet around those things.
- Pulled everything you learned together to create your unique personal style!

Ready to transform your style and stop second guessing yourself?
Live Your Life In Style is incredibly powerful and empowering work to begin our time together...
12 weeks 1:1
Let's do this work.
It's the high level container that will change not your business but your life.
DM me and say YES - I WANT PERSONAL STYLE SUCCESS! ... and lets chat

Message me on FB Messenger to inquire about coaching @m.me/dorrisburch

Free Resources

Manifesto: Grab your Fab Factor Self-Image Manifesto. Available @ TheFabFactor.com

Podcast: New Fab You Show with the fabulous Dorris Burch
This is a podcast for the woman who is ready to see yourself as the fabulous woman you are ... Say YES To Fabulous!

Don't miss an episode: NewFabYouShowPodcast.com
Subscribe and leave a review

Become A Fab Factor Brand Ambassador

If you believe that…

There is **Power** in the **Voice** in a Fabulous Woman… There is **Purpose** in the **Life** of a Fabulous Woman… There is **Passion** in the **Heart** of a Fabulous Woman…

Get your No Cost image at… BeFabulousImage.com

Website
TheFabFactor.com

Facebook Page
https://www.facebook.com/thefabfactoracademy

Instagram
@IAmTheFabulousDorrisBurch

ABOUT THE FABULOUS DORRIS BURCH

THE FABULOUS DORRIS BURCH is a thought shaker, style expert, fire brand, author, speaker, podcast hostess, remember who you always were, master life coach aligning women to elevate their self-image in the areas of Fabulous Mindset, Fabulous Style, Fabulous Surroundings. Through her weekly "New Fab You Show" podcast, and ongoing mastermind for women entrepreneurs, and compiler of the bestselling "Don't Be Invisible Be Fabulous" anthology book series, and her bestselling "The Little Black Book Of Being Fabulous" book, and her daily free inspirational posts, and videos distributed across her social media channels, she empowers women to be fabulous and design soul-led lives and businesses they are wildly obsessed with to live their most fabulous life. Her mission is to have women globally to Don't Be Invisible. Be Fabulous!

Combining a background in fashion and metaphysical science with practical life & business advice and a deep knowledge of spiritual and energetic principles, Fabulous Dorris isn't quite like any other "coach" you've encountered. A true self-made fabulous woman. She credits her success to her sheer determination, a deep desire to serve others, and an unwavering belief in her own dreams.

Fabulous Dorris has earned a master of public affairs in government/business relations, a master of arts in human resources & management and a bachelor of science in fashion merchandising and a bachelor's in metaphysical science. In addition to many many certifications in coaching and leadership.

She is a native of Kansas City, Missouri, but currently lives in the Chicagoland area with her husband and son.

Made in the USA
Monee, IL
12 July 2021

c8f26c57-e0e3-4fc1-8ce8-04671ca7eb40R02